Unexpected Calls to Unexpected Places:

SERMONS ON JONAH

by

WAYNE E. CROFT, SR., D.MIN., PH.D.

Foreword by

REV. OTIS MOSS III

R.H.Boyd
Publishing
CORPORATION
A GLOBAL NAME IN PUBLISHING FOR OVER 100 YEARS
~ R.H.Boyd Company

Printed by R.H. Boyd Publishing Corporation
Nashville, Tennessee

Unexpected Calls to Unexpected Places: Sermons on Jonah
Copyright © 2013 by R.H. Boyd Publishing Corporation, Nashville, TN

6717 Centennial Blvd.
Nashville, TN, 37209

ISBN 1-00000-000-0

Unless otherwise noted, all Scripture citations are from the *New Revised Standard Version of the Bible,* © 1989 by the Division of Christian Education of the National Council of Churches of Christ in the United States of America. Used by permission. All rights reserved.

Scripture quotations marked "NIV" are taken from *The Holy Bible, New International Version,* copyright ©1973, 1978, 1984, by the International Bible Society. Used by permission.

Printed in the United States of America

Wayne E. Croft, Sr., D.Min., Ph.D.
Unexpected Calls to Unexpected Places: Sermons on Jonah

TABLE OF CONTENTS

ACKNOWLEDGEMENTS

The writing of this book took place during a very difficult time in my pastoral ministry. For years, I had wanted to publish in book form what I have preached from the pulpit. This book was to serve as a gift to the people of The Church of the Redeemer Baptist in Philadelphia where I served as senior pastor for nineteen years. I, however, experienced an "unexpected call" to an "unexpected place" and ended my pastorate at Redeemer before this book was published. This book remains a gift to Redeemer but also now a gift of gratitude to the wonderful people who comprise the St. Paul's Baptist Church in West Chester, Pennsylvania, who listened to the voice of God and extended to me the call to be their pastor.

We are told, in the African-American preaching tradition, that sermons are to be heard and not read. One can miss all of the characteristics of African-American preaching when he or she does not witness this art with his or her own eyes and ears: characteristics such as call and response, ecstatic involvement, oral celebration (or "whooping"), intonation, physical gestures, and the like. However, in reading these sermons one will hopefully pick up on the strong biblical content, creative use of language, prophetic utterance, and alliteration that are also common characteristics in African-American preaching.

I know that this book would never have come to fruition without God's strength. I thank and acknowledge my Lord and Savior who called me to preach and entrusted me with the Gospel message. If I had any doubts about my need of the Lord, I no longer have any. I know that if it had not been for the Lord, this project would have never been completed and I would not be here today. There are so many that have helped shape this book so I want to thank everyone that has played a part in my life, lest I overlook anyone. To my first pair of theologians: my late father Deacon Rice Croft, who served as a deacon under my pastoral ministry until his death, and my mother, Deaconess Henrietta Croft, who recognized God's call on my life the day I was born. Thanks, Dad and Mom, for leading me to the Lord. I am also grateful for six siblings who have always supported me in ministry: Deacon Rose L. Holman, Rev. John A. Croft, Arlene Heath, Doreen Oveida, Elizabeth Johnson, and Rice R. Croft.

As the saying goes, no man [or woman] is an island. These sermons—and every sermon I preach—are the result of someone's influence in my life. There are numerous preacher friends who in different ways touched my life and shaped my preaching. To you, I say thank you: Rev. Roy M. Maddrey of the Enon Chapel Baptist Church in Philadelphia, who licensed me to the Gospel ministry at age twelve; Bishop Keith W. Reed, Sr., of Sharon Baptist Church in Philadelphia, who demonstrated strong biblical preaching and ordained me to the Gospel ministry; Rev. Dr. Jim Holley of the Historic Little Rock Baptist Church in Detroit, Michigan, who encouraged me to publish these sermons, made sure they were published, mentored me, and who still plays a significant role in my life; Rev. Dr. Albert F. Campbell of the Mount Carmel Baptist Church in Philadelphia, who is a father in the ministry and prays for me daily; the Dr. DeForest

"Buster" Soaries of First Baptist Church of Lincoln Gardens in Somerset, New Jersey, who mentored me through my first doctoral program from which I was honored to graduate as the only "Soaries Fellow"; Rev. Dr. Otis Moss III, of Trinity United Church of Christ in Chicago, Illinois; and Rev. Frank A. Thomas of Mississippi Boulevard Christian Church in Memphis, Tennessee, my accountability partners and friends; Rev. Dr. Damone B. Jones, Sr. of the Bible Way Baptist Church in Philadelphia; my nephew, Rev. Jermaine T. Heath, Sr., who listened to each of these sermons and encouraged me to publish them; and Rev. Semaj R. Vanzant, pastor of Christ United Methodist Church, Oklahoma City, Oklahoma, who also read and edited each one of these sermons. Any mistakes are mine and not his. Thanks, Semaj! To the R.H. Boyd Publishing Corporation, thank you for publishing this series of sermons.

Last, but not least, thanks belong to my children Darlene, Wayne, Jr., and Candace Nicole. Thank you for allowing me to be daddy. You have brought nothing but joy to my life and for that I am grateful. To my wife, Lisa, thank you for making sure I finished this endeavor. You gave me time and space without complaint and your love and support to see this through was unfailing. Your light continues to shine so brightly.

Without faith it is impossible to please God!

INTRODUCTION

When we talk about the story of Jonah, we immediately think about Jonah inside the fish. But the book of Jonah is really not about a fish. In fact, only three verses deal with Jonah's time inside the fish. The book of Jonah is really not even about the city of Nineveh, although what happened to Nineveh is a great testimony. The real focus of this short book is Jonah's own story. It is a story of disobedience, stubbornness, failure, success, racism, egotism, prayer, second chances, and—most of all—God's grace. Jonah's story is the story of someone like you and me. When we study the book of Jonah we come to realize that there is some of Jonah in all of us.

Jonah's book is found among the Minor Prophets, because of its short length. But Jonah is a minor prophet with a major message. What is the message of Jonah? We could pick out several, depending on the lens we use to interpret this narrative. One of the most important messages of Jonah is that God often calls us unexpectedly to go to unexpected places. The truth is our lives are often reshaped by these unexpected calls. The Bible itself is the story of how God unexpectedly breaks into the lives of people and sends them to unexpected places in order to shape them into the people God desires them to be.

One cannot read this series of sermons and not agree with the eighteenth-century hymnist, William Cowper, that God moves in a mysterious way.

We never know when God is going to call us and tell us to go somewhere we would rather not go. Yet we must always be ready to accept both the call and the assignment even when it comes as a surprise. If the call is to preach prophetically, we must. In my walk with the Lord, I have come to learn that what may be unexpected to us is never unexpected to God. On Sunday, May 13, 2012, at 2:17 P.M., I received a call informing me that I had been elected as Senior Pastor of the St. Paul's Baptist Church in West Chester, Pa. The journey to St. Paul's was unexpected. I had thought that I would conclude my pastoral ministry at the church I was presently serving. I had served there, in total, twenty years, both as interim and senior pastor. I began writing this book not knowing that God was calling me to serve elsewhere. It was for me an unexpected call to an unexpected place. Unlike Jonah, however, I knew it was God's will, so I did not go reluctantly but in total obedience.

As you read through this book of sermons, remember God who has called you is faithful and there is no place you can go where God is not. God not only calls us unexpectedly to go to unexpected places and proclaim His Word, but He also goes with us.

But now thus says the LORD, *he who created you, O Jacob, he who formed you, O Israel: Do not fear, for I have redeemed you; I have called you by name, you are mine. When you pass through the waters, I will be with you; and through the rivers, they shall not overwhelm you; when you walk through fire you shall not be burned, and the flame shall not consume you. For I am the* LORD *your God, the Holy One of Israel, your Savior.* (Isaiah 43:1-3)

FOREWORD

"The preacher is on one side an organ of his church, on the other a representative of his congregation according to his position."
Friedrich Schleiermacher (1768-1834)

"They seemed to be staring at the dark, but their eyes were watching God."
Zora Neale Hurston, *Their Eyes Were Watching God*

Preaching is a peculiar vocation where the minister stands in two worlds trying to reconcile apparent contradictions. On one hand, he stands as a representative of the Church, a priestly guide bringing the needs of the people before God. On the other hand, he is a prophetic force staring into the darkness, naming tragedy, and pointing to triumph through the abyss.

Dr. Wayne E. Croft, Sr., preacher, pastor, husband, father, son, and friend, stands comfortably in the intersection of priestly concerns and prophetic calling. His decade-plus service to the people of God has been a pastorate of hope and healing. I have watched Pastor Croft preach with a rare sense of urgency and commitment. His messages never shun the reality of darkness, nor do they leave the hearer with a shallow sense of hope. He is careful to mine the text as an archaeologist of the biblical landscape and frame his ancient discoveries with modern apparel to ensure the congregation recognizes the biblical terrain far removed from where he proclaims.

The joy of hearing a Croft sermon is to catch a glimpse of a young man burdened with the weight of preaching. One can sense the press of the Spirit forcing him to ingest the narrative and embody it, not just recite the words. His entire being becomes possessed by what homiletician Jana Childers calls "holy performance." This is in no way to suggest what one witnesses is a false act, but rather a profound incarnation of mind, body, and spirit reshaped to act as a public witness of the Gospel.

All of his senses are engaged. His mind meticulously frames the text and proposition. His heart connects with the grand, but elusive, ideas of love, hope, and faith as the Spirit weaves it all together. The greatest form of preaching in the African-American tradition is incarnational preaching, where the head and heart are engaged to communicate the sacred. Wayne Croft not only preaches with incarnational power, but fuses that power with a postmodern sensibility that allows the unchurched and formerly churched to hear the Gospel in new and powerful ways. Very few ministers truly have this gift of evangelical witness, prophetic zeal, and sensitivity for the unchurched. Reverend Dr. Wayne E. Croft, Sr. is one of the models of this method of preaching. This collection of sermons on Jonah will be a treat to all. Those who love the Church and those who have left the Church will find strength and hope as Dr. Croft masterfully pierces the darkness and shows us how to watch God through our storms.

Asking you to imagine,

The Rev. Dr. Otis Moss III, Senior Pastor
Trinity United Church of Christ, Chicago, Illinois

Chapter One

PREACHING JONAH AND PROPHETIC PREACHING IN THE AFRICAN-AMERICAN TRADITION

*W*hen one analyzes the African-American[1] preaching tradition one will notice that it has traditionally concerned itself with social conditions and has emphasized hope. It appears that most of the preaching in the African-American community today, however, stresses individualism and personal achievement. As a result, the aim of preaching is to change individuals rather than institutions or society as a whole. The truth is, of course, preaching must be concerned about both the individual and society. Marvin McMickle, in his book *Where Have All the Prophets Gone?*, argues that what we know as prophetic preaching has suffered a decline over the last twenty-five years.[2] Prophetic preaching can be found throughout the Bible, in the words of the Hebrew prophets and in the preaching of Jesus Christ. The origins of prophetic preaching in our own era—and specifically in the African-American church—can be found in the 1960s with the civil rights movement, the antiwar movement, the student non-violent movement, the women's rights movement, and the war on poverty.

The black church during this era proudly proclaimed that when the government needed an institution to assist them with social concerns their first call was often to the black church. This, unfortunately, has progressively changed. Today there are many critics who contend that mainline Protestant preaching has grown silent on public affairs and, at the same time, has also failed to meet the needs of the individuals who fill our pews. To take one example, according to a 1988 study of preaching in the Christian Church (Disciples of Christ), done by sociologist Joseph Faulkner of Pennsylvania State University, only five percent of the 206 sermons he evaluated dealt with social issues.[3]

Although this study was completed twenty-four years ago, not much has changed. Today God is often spoken of as a cosmic therapist who helps people deal with their individual lives and alleviates psychological burdens, such as guilt or self-doubt.[4] No doubt we need this type of preaching. Dr. Cleophus J. LaRue, in his book, *The Heart of Black Preaching*, states that one of the five "domains of experience" to which black preaching speaks is care of the soul:

> "Care of the soul describes that area of experience that focuses on the well-being of individuals. It is, however, more than mere comfort for the bereaved, forgiveness for the guilty, and help for the sick and needy; it is preeminently the renewal of life in the image of Christ. Thus it has as its purpose not only the giving of comfort but also the redirection of life. The preaching that grows out of reflection on this domain concerns itself with the healing, sustaining, guiding, and reconciling of persons as they face the changes and challenges of common human experiences, experiences that are exacerbated in

black life through systemic and capricious discrimination and prejudice."[5]

In 1963, Dr. Martin Luther King, Jr. published a book of sermons titled *Strength to Love.* In a sermon called "A knock at midnight," he acknowledged the popularity of preaching that solely focuses on individuals. King observed, "Bestsellers in religion are such books as *Peace of Mind* and *Peace of Soul.* The popular clergyman preaches soothing sermons on 'How to be Happy' and 'How to Relax.' Some have been tempted to revise Jesus' command to read, 'Go ye into all the world, keep your blood pressure down, and, lo, I will make you a well-adjusted personality.'"[6] For many people, the counselor has replaced the clergyperson and the clinic has replaced the Church. Such preaching assumes that Christian faith is intended to help people cope with the world as it is because the world is going to persist much as it is now. To be clear, our preaching must be concerned with the lives of the people who gather to listen week after week for a word from the Lord. However, we must also employ a prophetic word as well. The God of the Bible seeks not simply to help us survive a difficult world but aims to remake the world so that His divine purposes are manifest in all things.

In the face of so many national and global problems—war in Iraq and Afghanistan, genocide in Africa, devastation of land in New Orleans and in Haiti, overcrowded prisons, drug abuse, lack of medical insurance and quality public education, racism, and sexism—there is a desperate need for prophetic preaching as well as preaching from prophetic books. Dr. Samuel Dewitt Proctor, in his article "Prophetic Preaching Now: A Generation after King," contends, "The faith of Black people delivered them from their oppression and wafted their souls in realms eternal. And the one who led them in this experience was the preacher, the one called to stand between their travail and their God."[7] Dr. Proctor further argues that we need preachers to inspire those who have given up, to stir up their pride and respect. Too many of our preachers, he writes, are not calling people to discipline and devotion. They are preaching a soft message of materialism and selfish regard. Services are dominated by a focus on what God gives us, not what we give in service and devotion. It is a gospel of 'give me' and not a message of 'use me.' It is all 'Thank you Jesus,' and 'thank you, Lord, for what you have done for me.' Proctor argues that this is not prophetic preaching. Indeed, it is barely preaching at all.[8]

The Church must be challenged on issues that confront our society. Preachers must be challenged to go places—unexpected places—and preach biblically and prophetically and neither one needs to be distinct. The Church stands in need of prophets in a problem-filled world, prophets who not only speak truth to power, but truth to the powerless as well. There is a need for prophetic preaching and for preachers who will stand up, rise up, and challenge the injustices of this world.

The question for some, at this point, may be: What is prophetic preaching? There is much confusion about the true nature and purpose of prophetic preaching and what it means to preach from the prophetic books. Phrases such as "preaching on social issues," "preaching on controversial issues," and "preaching for social transformation" are often used in an inclusive sense as a rough equivalent for prophetic preaching in homiletical circles. In his book *Speaking the Truth in Love,* Christian ethicist J. Philip Wogaman defines prophetic preaching as preaching that "draws people into the reality of God in such a way that they cannot any longer be content with conventional wisdom and superficial existence."[9]

The homiletician Ronald J. Allen defines prophetic preaching as a "mode of bearing witness to the grace of God which seeks to correct some aspect of the community's understanding of God, of the vocation or the life of the community or its perception of the world."[10] The late Kelly Miller Smith, in *Social Crisis Preaching,* defines it as "...the proclamation of that which is crucially relevant within the context of the Christian gospel in times of social upheaval and stress. It aims at setting corrective measures into motion."[11] More recently, Marvin A. McMickle simply defines prophetic preaching as biblical speech concerning justice and righteousness.[12] Thus prophetic preaching is a homiletical mode of proclaiming the Word of God to a community that helps it to recover its ethical relationship to God, respond to critical challenges for social transformation, and embrace an eschatological vision of God's future.

But there is another question that must be considered when preaching prophetically: What is postmodernity? We preach in a new world, a world very different from the one inhabited by the prophets. In the twenty-first century, postmodernism has almost become a household word. Information about this concept is plentiful as many have developed their own definition for it based on their respective disciplines. Sometime around the turn of the seventeenth century, there began what is often called the modern period. It lasted, roughly, until sometime in the late twentieth century. The vigorous youth of this period is known as the Enlightenment, a time marked by the intellectual and philosophical conviction that truth could only be obtained through the powers of human reason, observation, and experiment. The Enlightenment lasted, more or less, from 1650 to 1750, but set the tone for the centuries that followed. In Europe and North America, these last two centuries have been a time in which people turned to science and its promises in order to fill a void left by a decline in religion. Knowledge was viewed as certain, objective, and good. The stage beyond modernity has become known as postmodernity, the contemporary intellectual and cultural stage that is marked by a rejection of "objective truth" and skepticism about the power of reason and claims of universality. These have been replaced by a corporate understanding of truth that is relative to each community in which one participates.[13]

You will often hear the words *secular, pluralistic,* and *contemporary* used as if they are the same as postmodern. They are not. As Sarah Asaftei points out:

- "A secular person is mainly viewed as one who does not believe in God.
- A pluralist believes in many gods or truths.
- A contemporary person is merely someone living in the same time period as you and me.
- A postmodern individual is more complex. They don't necessarily deny God; they just don't have a growing relationship with God. They don't reject truth; they just aren't sure where to find it."[14]

There are indeed many postmodernities. Responses to postmodernism generally fall into two camps: one of uncritical acceptance, the other of strong aversion. However, whether we like it or not the world we are called to preach in is rapidly changing and appears to be shifting from a modern mentality to a postmodern one.

Can we preach from the prophetic books and draw together both the individual and society? Since prophetic preaching is concerned with social ills and injustice, how do we preach prophetically in a world that simply says, "Make me holla," or "Tell me it's my season and year for a breakthrough"? How do we preach prophetically in a world where everyone simply wants to be blessed and highly favored? In other words, how do we preach prophetically in a society that is more individualistic than communal? Furthermore, what does it take to preach prophetically in a world that is more interested in a prosperity theology rather than a prophetic one or one in which the prophetic books, both major and minor, are rarely preached? This takes us back to our earlier question: How do we preach prophetically in a postmodern world?

I believe postmodernism presents Christian preachers with new challenges and rich opportunities. Today people are looking for new answers and the Church is afforded a new opportunity to knock on the door and present its case. Diogenes Allen writes, "A culture that is increasingly free of the assumptions of the Enlightenment view of science, religion, morality, and society is a culture that is increasingly free of assumptions that prevent one from coming to an appreciation of the intellectual strength of Christianity."[15] The challenge, however, is that the Church cannot silence other beliefs but must now sit with other faiths at the world's table and declare its message. It must be willing to "compete" for authority and share the world's stage. Christians are no longer the dominant presence at the table. Muslims, Jews, Buddhists, New Agers, Hindus, and many others are there as well. We, however, must not come to the table with a spirit of timidity when asked to address social injustice.

But neither can we come with a spirit of triumphalism. This sharing at the table, however, with other beliefs and faiths is not new. In the Bible patriarchs, matriarchs, prophets, and prophetesses had to do the same.

- Abraham had to share the table with people who worshiped the Sumerian god Nanna.
- Joshua had to give Israel a choice between serving God or the gods their fathers served on the other side of the river and in Egypt (see Josh. 24).
- After Gideon died, Israel turned to Baal-berit (see Judg. 8:33).
- Elijah had to interact with Ahab and Jezebel who served Baal (see 1 Kings 16:29-33).
- Amos had to interact with those who served the god Chiun (see Amos 5:26, KJV).
- The men of Cuth worshiped Nergal (see 2 Kings 17:30).

Although at one time Christianity was unquestionably the dominant religion in the West, today it must share the table and it must come to that table with epistemological humility. Preaching in a postmodern world must recognize and acknowledge its ambiguities. It must see its voice as only one voice that is surrounded by many other voices. It, however, must tell the whole truth and nothing but the truth while understanding that its truth will be received by some as being limited. We see through a glass dimly. Our encounters with other faiths will only increase. At the same time, though, our faith need not be considered inferior by its practitioners or adversaries.

Postmodern preaching does not afford us the luxury that modern preaching had or at least seemed to once possess. At one time, we could claim certain things to be clear and obvious to everyone who had the ability to understand. It was a rather epistemologically exclusive claim. Today, however, postmoderns offer questions and challenging alternatives that must be considered by the effective preacher. This is especially true when preaching from the book of Jonah. There are elements in this prophetic book that have led some to view it a myth or fable. Jonah's interaction with the fish raises questions about the credibility of such a tale. One must wrestle with and preach such texts and narratives always prepared to engage in dialogue with others who may have questions about their validity.

One of the defining characteristics of postmodernism is the proliferation of choices and options. "Postmodernists view this abundance of choices as needed and liberating."[16] They want to enter into conversation. They want to feel free to argue with what we preach or claim as truth. They want to see whether or not the preacher is upset, struggling, or has difficulty with controversial passages in the Bible in a way that correlates with what they struggle with in the world. No other form of preaching does this, but prophetic preaching does. It struggles and wrestles with the text and with what it sees going on in the world. It brings the text to the people, so that the pew and pulpit can wrestle with the text together.

In order for this to happen the text must not be taken out of context. The popularity and growth of prosperity preaching requires prophetic preachers to be doctrinally sound, theologically grounded, and socially relevant. Unfortunately, it appears that today's pulpit has not taken theological reflection seriously. This may be the reason why we hear less preaching from the prophetic books. Prophetic books challenge us to go deep into the context to understand the author's original intent and context. What we hear preached in many of our pulpits today does not require much exegesis or thought. Our failure to address public issues theologically has left preaching without a clear mission and focus. In an age that has neglected theology, preaching has prioritized personal concerns such as pastoral care, teaching, edification, and counseling. While these are important, we must also proclaim God's concern for the marginalized and oppressed and our concern for the "least of these." Furthermore we cannot resist going, like Jonah, to places where God sends us and preaching prophetically, pastorally, and theologically. Preaching must be undergirded with sound theology. In his book, *A Captive Voice*, David Buttrick encourages preachers to turn back once more to theology and learn to think theologically:

"Preaching does not merely interpret biblical texts; preaching is a ministry of meaning, and meaning in the midst of our confusing world is surely a pulpit vocation; we must help congregations to discern the times. Theology articulates faith in contemporary language and in relation to contemporary structure of thought. If preaching is to interpret what is going on, then it must think theologically over events and issues."[17]

Another defining characteristic of postmodernism that will challenge the prophetic preacher is its relentless questioning of authority. In the early third century A.D., Tertullian denied the use of the Bible to any who did not teach what had become the faith advocated by the Church. With that decision, the orthodox church in effect claimed exclusive authority to read and interpret the Scriptures. Officials of the church interpreted the Bible for the masses, and the church's word held sole authority. The Bible remained the church's book for the most part, but humanism and the Reformation challenged this authority. Martin Luther's doctrine of *sola Scriptura* claimed the right of the individual believer to interpret Scripture for him- or herself.

The contest over the right to interpret Scripture was really a way-station to modernism, halfway between the premodern and modern worlds. Under *sola Scriptura*, the Bible remained an unquestioned authority. It did not remain so as the modern period wore on. If conscientious individuals could question the Church's traditional interpretations of the Bible, could they not question the claims of the Bible itself? Although in reality no one can interpret the Bible using *sola Scriptura* exclusively, this thread ran through the changes in Christian history and led us to postmodernism's radical questioning of all authority.[18] How can we proclaim "Thus saith the LORD" like the prophets in a world that questions authority?

Unless I am mistaken, within most African-American Christian contexts, the Bible remains authoritative. What makes the Bible authoritative in the African-American preaching tradition, according to Cleophus LaRue, is that it speaks to the conditions of African Americans:

"There is in black preaching a high regard for Scripture. Black preaching has historically been noted for its strong biblical content. In many black churches, biblical preaching, defined as preaching that allows a text from the Bible to serve as the leading force in shaping the content and purpose of the sermon, is the type of preaching considered to be most faithful to traditional understandings of the proclaimed Word."[19]

In the homiletical debate concerning what is distinctive in the black preaching tradition, scholars have argued for a range of distinctive characteristics. While these characteristics inevitably overlap to some degree, they can be grouped under the headings of rhetorical and theological characteristics. Rhetorically, black preaching is marked by four stylistic traits: rhythm and musical sound, call and response, poetic language and imagery, and storytelling. Theologically, black preaching assumes (1) a hermeneutic rooted in the sovereignty of God and (2) a hermeneutic rooted in celebration. We find these assumptions woven into the sermons I have written on Jonah.

A hermeneutic rooted in the sovereignty of God is what I believe makes the Bible authoritative in African-American preaching. LaRue contends that at the center of powerful black preaching is a hermeneutic that views God as sovereignly acting on behalf of dispossessed and marginalized people: "Indeed, it is no secret that the Bible occupies a central place in the religious life of black Americans. More than a mere source for texts, it is the single most important source of language, imagery, and story for the black sermon."[21] Why is this? Blacks find in the Bible a God who hears the cry of the people and calls for the liberation of the captives.

The biblical narratives are not foreign to the black experience. Blacks see a strong connection between their history and the Israelites' Exodus experience. Each is a set of stories about a community that suffers brutal oppression and yet is sustained by faith and by its hope for freedom that is promised and ultimately delivered. YHWH is viewed as a Liberator of the oppressed and Jesus in the New Testament is viewed similarly.[22] These biblical stories carry authority in black life and culture because they ring so true to the reality lived out by the listeners, those who thirst for truth in world otherwise governed by lies and betrayal. African Americans trust the Word of God because it has been dependable as a way out of no way, offering hope in hopeless situations. The truth of the text is grasped when it is confirmed in the life story of a person or community with whom they can identify.[23]

The reason the prophets of old were effective was their commitment to speaking God's truth within their context. Abraham Heschel and Walter Brueggemann, throughout their writing on the prophets, consistently name this truth.[24] They, along with other scholars, confirm that prophets spoke to their own people during their time with a relevant message and they did it whether people liked it or not. They prepared their messages with their listeners in mind. They were in touch with the heart of God and the spiritual condition of the people. This was a defining characteristic of the prophets, those who spoke to the times of the people and who declared justice for God's people.

With this defining characteristic, one can understand why African-American youth today do not name Elijah, Isaiah, Jeremiah, Amos, or Jonah as prophets, but rather Tupac, Lauryn Hill, Ludacris, Kanye West, Common, Jay Z, and others. These hip-hop artists have spoken to the context of urban youth. The hip-hop generation has stated that in church they have heard the right story but in the wrong language. They have heard it in the *King James Version*, the *New*

International Version, the *New Revised Standard Version* and the like, but biblical narratives have not been explained within their context and made relevant to their struggles. Church youth, regardless of ethnicity, are influenced by hip-hop because it relates to their existential experience. Hip-hop "has risen from its inner-city roots to influence youth from the American suburbs to Tokyo."[25] My children are preacher's kids and they have been influenced by hip-hop. One cannot talk about preaching prophetically and not preach to the context of his or her listeners. During a televised benefit concert for Hurricane Katrina victims, Kanye West did what prophets do: he named the oppressor publicly. After New Orleans received what many believe was a lack of support from the Bush administration, Kanye exclaimed, "George Bush doesn't care about Black people." Producer Rick Kaplan immediately cut off West's microphone, but his comment still reached much of the United States.[26] He was viewed as a prophet by the hip-hop generation.

In 2006, the hip-hop artist known as Ludacris released a song in which he took a bold stand against domestic abuse, the devastating effects of chemical dependency, violence, and so many other tragic aspects of youth culture. His willingness to speak through rap on these issues has, for many of our youth, earned him the title of prophet. "Hip-hop has used rap to tell stories of urban youth, poverty, oppression, inner-city life, anger and African-American history."[27] Some hip-hop artists have been viewed as socially conscious emcees who have educated their listeners about what's going on in urban culture. They have talked about how to improve one's life through workshops and discussions. They have condemned injustice, but they have also connected to the lives of their listeners by speaking—sometimes positively and sometimes negatively—in the language of their listeners. And, because of their willingness to speak out they have been named "The Prophets of Hip-Hop."

This is what postmodern prophetic preaching must do today. Although I can't rap or battle as one of God's prophets, I must craft a message from God that is relevant to both young and old. Listeners must be invited to hear stories of people with whom they can connect in order to grasp the truth of the text. I believe the book of Jonah provides us with an enormous opportunity to connect a text with the lived experience of both our listeners and the preacher. It also reminds us that we have failed to look at what James and Christine Ward calls the "wider dimensions" of justice and righteousness.[28]

The challenge for the African-American church in this postmodern world is not so much an outright rejection of biblical authority as a suspicion of answers that seem too simplistic. Graham Johnston observes,

"The real issue is not one of an inerrant text, as much as having any authoritative text at all. The issue is no longer about what is in the text or what the original author intended but about what is in the interpretation of the text as understood by the present-day reader. The postmodern mistrust of words and texts will put new pressure on the field of hermeneutics, particularly at the professional theological level ... People in a postmodern context are unprepared to trust something without first being able to examine and probe its reliability."[29]

The Bible, however, can be both authoritative and relevant in a postmodern context because it can reach out to and meet people where they are. Thus, preaching must take the Bible and—in the African-American expression—"make it live" and "tell the story." The cry from the pew to the preacher is, "Preacher, paint the picture." Preaching must make the text live, tell the story, and paint the picture. Unfortunately, this generation is said to be the most biblically illiterate generation: many people simply don't know the story. They have named, claimed, proclaimed, and re-arranged Scriptures that speak of prosperity. But rarely, if at all, are they familiar with the prophetic words of Isaiah, Jeremiah, Amos, Jonah, Jesus, and others. Thus preaching from the prophetic books, whether major or minor, is needed to re-introduce a biblically illiterate generation to the whole Gospel. Our preaching must bring a word from the Lord through an ancient text and that text must bring meaning to the lives of those who listen. I believe preaching from the book of Jonah allow us to do this.

James Melvin Washington, in his book, *Frustrated Fellowship*, calls us "stalkers after meaning."[30] People are looking for meaning in life. Since science and technology have failed in the postmodern view, the preacher has a chance to come to the table and offer meaning to those who are seeking answers to life—not only to the individual but to the community as well. People are looking inward for truth. In postmodern society, truth is an internal construct rather than an external reality. Because people have so many options when it pertains to truth, preaching must be honest. It cannot simply proclaim a gospel of health and wealth. Rather, it must also preach an honest gospel concerning our responsibility for those in Nineveh. It must tell of the tension between theology and reality and the distance that is often felt between dust and deity. But it must not be so relevant that it is no longer incarnational. In other words, it must not be so dumbed down that one cannot see Jesus. For the cry still comes from the pew and from many in the world, "Sir [or ma'am], we would see Jesus." Preaching from the prophetic books must help a world that is lost to see Jesus. It must connect what God said over two thousand years ago to what the world and people in it are experiencing today. Prophetic preaching must take the text, uplift the context, and help people live out the right conduct.

Every Sunday, at the St. Paul's Baptist Church in West Chester, Pennsylvania, I preach to postmodernist "stalkers after meaning," as well as to moderns who hold fast to traditions and the promise of hope and help. The question that I ask myself is: What should be the word for the people today? Who are the people in the pews? I have found that the word needs to be one of encouragement regardless of who is in the pew. For postmodernists particularly, a sermon that does not force, push, or coerce them but keeps them thinking about life and its complexities will keep them coming back. If there remain those who are hungry for a word from the Lord, what keeps us from preaching sound, biblical, and relevant sermons?

There are at least two reasons why some preachers neglect prophetic preaching or preaching from the prophetic books. First, some preachers view such preaching as appropriate only with regard to the ancient prophetic books. They see it as an ancient style of preaching. Preaching prophetically from the Bible, however, is not limited to the prophetic books. One can preach prophetically from the entire canon.

Consider Psalm 73. Asaph had numerous questions and concerns about the society in which he lived. Asaph witnessed the arrogant and wicked prospering, not struggling with the cares of this world. He saw them walking around with strong and healthy bodies, free from the burdens common to humankind, not plagued by human ills. He saw that they had pride as their necklace, they clothed themselves with violence, their hearts were callous and filled with iniquity, and their minds consumed with evil. Asaph witnessed all of this going on in a world in which God reigned. Because of this, he said that his trust in God almost failed. He had questions for God but no answers for the people that confronted him about the justice of God. People in the pew today, like Asaph, look at the state of this world and the injustices of life and wonder: Where is God? Asaph, however, said when he went into the sanctuary of God, he understood the final destiny of the wicked. Although this text is not from one of the prophetic books, it is not foreign to what we see happening. Though ancient, it proclaims God's ultimate justice in a way that contemporary readers can recognize.

Second, preaching from prophetic books has most frequently been equated with judgmental preaching that is filled with anger, indignation, and condemnation. If we view the prophetic books and prophetic preaching in this manner, such preaching will seem to smack of pretentiousness, moral self-righteousness, or even soothsaying. However, we miss the real meaning of the prophetic books if that is all we see. The prophets have been regarded as social reformers, preachers of ethics, or astute political observers who condemned the ways of Israelite society on the basis of absolute standards of justice and righteousness. The hallmark of the prophet is this message. For this reason, prophetic preaching might be called corrective preaching. This view is certainly justified on the basis of the prophets' choice of words such as *woe* and *repent*. To be sure, preaching from the prophetic books, in part, includes proclaiming words first heard in historical settings that were quite unlike our own, criticizing social injustice, and exhorting people to social action. When it is seen in its fullness, however, prophetic preaching is not an out-of-date phenomenon belonging to past cultures nor can it be caricatured as an angry and a judgmental voice toward the community.

Although many of us can relate to prophets like Jonah, the nature and continuing significance of prophetic preaching for the Church today cannot simply involve mimicking the Hebrew prophets. Preachers today must continue to speak out against injustice with love and, having been convicted, hold themselves and their hearers accountable for their actions as Jonah did in his book. This same preacher must be willing to go where God sends him or her with this message. Sometimes the preacher-prophet will receive an unexpected call to an unexpected place to preach God's Word and to do it without hesitation. James and Christine Ward have observed that there are many reasons why believers resist the call of God like Jonah. Jeremiah struggled with his call because he felt inadequate. Sarah doubted her call to bear a child because of her barrenness and advanced age. Moses resisted God's call because of the enormity of the task. Jonah, however, does not resist his call because of discouragement, failure to trust God, or stubbornness. Jonah resists because he detests the Ninevites. Because of his own prejudices, he wants them destroyed. He resists God's call to ministry and preaching because he refuses to be an instrument of God's love for a people he despises.[31] Nevertheless, God still brings hope to a hopeless people. Bringing hope to hopeless situations is a key part of genuine prophetic preaching.

In preaching, there must be a message of hope. This hope becomes the meaning of life for which postmoderns hunger. In a discussion of hope and the role it played in Israel's history, Walter Brueggemann asserts that "memories enable [a] community to hope against all data and to believe that the *hopelessness* of the data never rules out a different *possibility*. God can indeed work newness against all of the data. God can shatter the known world in order to establish a new historical possibility."[32] Thus in spite of what is going on in the world today, for the preacher, hope remains at the center of the Gospel of Jesus Christ and therefore at the center of Christian theology. There is hope for the preacher who is sent and for the listener. It's a hope that is grounded in an intrinsic relationship between God and God's action. J. Philip Wogaman states "Prophetic preaching deals not only with problems and evils to be overcome; it offers hope that they *can* be overcome."[33]

The motif of hope has an integral part in the African-American preaching tradition. Theologian James Cone acknowledges this in his book, *Black Theology and Black Power* (1969). In a new edition of this seminal work, Cone reviews some of the major trends and developments in black theology from 1969 to 1998. Cone initiates a serious critique of Western theological traditions and reinterprets Christianity through the lens of the African-American struggle for freedom, justice, and equality. Cone attempts to identify liberation as the heart of the Christian Gospel, and blackness as the primary mode of God's presence. What he says is relevant to Jonah because the oppressed and the oppressor meet in

Nineveh. Cone addresses powerless blacks with a Christian Gospel which liberates those who are oppressed and threatened by the power of their oppressors. He bases much of his theology on God's deliverance of Israel from oppression under the Egyptians and argues that this same God works for the deliverance of oppressed blacks. Cone further argues that the resurrection of Jesus symbolizes universal freedom for all and provides hope in the midst of oppression.[34]

Hope plays a vital role in Cone's theology. He states that black theology is a theology of hope for this life. The appeal to the next life only reflects a lack of hope. Hope, in Cone's theology, is not simply future reality. It is a present one that struggles for justice, humanizing of individuals, socializing of humanity, and peace for all creation today as well as in the world to come.[35] In defining hope, Cone says, "...hope is not a theoretical concept to be answered in a seminary classroom or in the privacy of one's experiences. It is a practical idea which deals with the reality of this world."[36] Even when we have gone in the opposite direction, like Jonah, due to our reluctance to preach to the marginalized, there is still hope, hope that God will not give up on us or the people we are called to inspire. The hope we find in the book of Jonah both for Jonah and the Ninevites is the hallmark of African-American preaching.

Homileticians have recognized the motif of hope to be an integral part of black preaching. I attempt to fill the sermons found in this book with hope. William B. McClain, in *Come Sunday: The Liturgy of Zion*, claims that what is distinctive in African-American preaching is no single rhetorical mode or theological theme but the confluence of ten different elements. These elements are biblical emphasis, prophetic

rather than pastoral preaching, poetic delivery, dialogue between pastor and people, didactic as well as inspiring, declar-
ative rather than suggestive preaching, slow and deliberate
build-up, dramatic pause, life-situational preaching, and
hope.[37] McClain highlights *hope* as an essential element of
African-American preaching: "No matter how dark a picture
has been painted or how gloomy, there is always a 'but' or a
'nevertheless' or an element in the climax of the sermon that
suggests holding on, marching forward, going through, or
overcoming."[38]

Cleophus J. LaRue implies that behind the veil of God's
sovereign involvement in the everyday affairs of black existence is the experience and expression of hope.[39] He unpacks
this assumption about the constitutive nature of hope during an interview with Lydia Talbot, concerning a sermon he
preached from the book of Habakkuk. LaRue says,

"[Anticipation] is hope born of experience because
when you preach about hope and a brighter tomorrow,
it is not something blacks are not acquainted with. We
have known this, we have seen this. So in a sense I am
simply reaffirming for them [the listeners] what they
already know and believe. If I were actually in front of
a black audience, they would be saying, 'Yes! Amen! We
know about what you are saying! We have lived it and
experienced this anticipation.'"[40]

LaRue views black preaching as originating in a context of
marginalization and struggle: "It is the interaction of marginalized black experience and biblical interpretation that
enables blacks to confront biblical texts in a compelling and
creative manner."[41] Thus, it is the sovereignty of God seen in
these biblical stories that gives rise to the motif of hope in

black preaching. LaRue writes, "What became important for blacks was the telling and retelling, the hearing and rehearing of biblical stories—stories that told of perseverance, of strength in weakness, and of hope in hopeless situations."[42] The motif of hope in black preaching, according to LaRue, is rooted in the mighty acts of God who responds on behalf of the marginalized and oppressed.

Henry H. Mitchell argues that in black preaching, hope elicits celebration. Celebration here is to be considered a theological instead of a rhetorical characteristic of black preaching since it is specifically celebrating God's liberating power. The cause of the celebration therefore is based upon hope in God's liberating power:

> "All humanity needs hope, but none so much as those who have so little other than hope. As the areas in which Black people can take up cudgels for themselves expand, their desperate need for hope may appear to diminish. But they will not soon be in the position to be numerically and physically in control, or even guaranteed justice, saved by the hope that is in their faith."[43]

For Mitchell, hope is evidenced in celebration and celebration is rooted in the hope heard in the prophetic tradition. Mitchell believes that the motif of hope is so essential that it must be proclaimed to oppressed people. According to Mitchell, "The sermon that celebrates without giving help is an opiate. The sermon that tries to help without celebration is, at least in the Black church, ineffective."[44]

Too often in preaching, the hope that we have is presented as solely eschatological. We see Christian hope as related only to the end of time or the life beyond. This kind of preaching tells postmoderns that things will work out in the end. This perspective is not entirely off base, but Christian hope is more than expecting everything to finally work out. It has something to add to everyday life. It is an inaugurated eschatology. It is an assurance that God is present in the world and involved in the lives of His people now to bring meaning, wholeness, and peace to a world crippled by despair. Prophetic preaching should proclaim the truth that we can find meaning, significance, and hope in life now not just "when we all get to heaven."

Postmodernism may never be accurately defined. Nevertheless, this is the context in which we live and where we must preach the Good News. It questions authority, searches for meaning, thirsts for knowledge, questions "the truth," and hungers for hope. The Gospel message, however, has before it the opportunity to meet the need and fulfill the hunger of postmodernism by presenting its story, claim, and hope. Although it is a message that is surrounded by other voices that claim to be telling the truth, it has just as many witnesses who have lived out and experienced its truth, realizing that those who hope in God are never put to shame. Prophetic preachers will encounter those both inside and outside churches who will attempt to silence them. When this happens, however, the prophet will not be on unfamiliar terrain. Prophets always have their opponents:

- Moses had the pharaoh.
- Elijah had Ahab.
- Esther had Haman.
- Jeremiah had Hananiah (see Jer. 28).
- Nehemiah had Sanballat.
- Ida B. Wells had the Chesapeake & Ohio Railroad.

- Mahatma Gandhi had Nathuram Godse.
- Rosa Parks had the Montgomery Bus Authorities.
- Martin Luther King, Jr. had J. Edgar Hoover and Bull Connor.
- Dietrich Bonhoeffer had Adolf Hitler.

Paul had Nero, and Jesus had Caiphas, Pilate, Herod, and oftentimes, His own people. In spite of the hostility, hatred, and ill regard, prophets must still proclaim, "Thus saith the LORD."

In the midst of war, genocide, injustice, the AIDS crisis, overcrowded prisons, racism, sexism, black on black crime, and so much more, the preacher's voice is needed more now than ever before. There is a "Help Wanted" ad in the pages of society that reads, "Preacher-Prophets needed to proclaim a message of hope to a world that desires justice."

Preachers cannot allow the injustices of this world to silence their voice. The world needs prophets in this postmodern world to speak into the lives of people and to this world in order to bring about repentance. Jonah speaks to us today. His problems are our problems: extreme nationalism, the denial of loving community and the quest for humane treatment, the problems of cultural and racial relationships, rebellion against God and the resulting storms. Jonah teaches us, as I try to show in this series of sermons, that God's love, grace, and mercy are available to all, even to those who try to run from God.[45] God's grace reaches out to a lost world, bringing hope and causing celebration. Although many view the prophetic books as narratives of doom and gloom, the book of Jonah concludes with a lost nation and her prophet experiencing the compassion of God. The book's message, then, is one not only of hope, which is the hallmark of

African-American preaching, but also one of celebration.

Celebration evokes a sense of enjoyment, enthusiasm, ecstasy, transcendence, adoration, and edification. The Gospel empowers the listener and offers him or her Good News in the midst of despairing times. In his book, *The Recovery of Preaching*, Henry H. Mitchell argues that "the genius of black preaching has been its capacity to generate this very kind of celebration, despite the hardest circumstances...."[46] In the most authentic forms of black preaching, there must be celebration, or what Mitchell calls "climactic utterance." The celebrant recognizes the goodness of God as seen in the text. Mitchell further suggests "...Those who do not know how to celebrate should learn the art... selfhood is validated, identity is reinforced, and the courage-to-be is renewed in the accepting, healing, uplifting presence of God."[47] The book of Jonah gives its readers and the preacher a reason to celebrate. A prophet and a nation have repented, Nineveh has experienced the compassion of God, and God's love is shown to not have any boundaries. Jonah gives us a reason to celebrate at the end of each of chapter.

The celebratory moment generally comes at the end of the sermon, but it can occur at any point in the sermon, since hope is always being proclaimed in black preaching.[48] Frank Thomas follows Mitchell in arguing that "celebration in the final stage of the sermon functions as the joyful, ecstatic reinforcement of the truth already taught and delivered in the main body of the sermon."[49]

Mitchell further observes, "Celebration dramatizes the main idea of the sermon and supports the behavioral purpose or motivational goal. The function could be called 'ecstatic reinforcement.' People relate to and remember what they celebrate, and it influences their behavior."[50] Black preaching exemplifies this and attempts to celebrate the good news that is found in the text. The book of Jonah provides us with enough good news to celebrate. A prophet has turned back to God after trying to flee His call and the Ninevites experience grace in its fullest expression. We, like Jonah, cannot escape from God and His call. God may call us unexpectedly to go to some unexpected place, but He does not send us without a word or without His power.

We can preach prophetically in a postmodern world knowing there is always hope even in the worst circumstances. In the words of the saints of old, "*There's a bright side somewhere.*" "Hark the voice of Jesus calling, 'Who will go and work today? Fields are white and harvest waiting. Who will bear the sheaves away?' Yes, there's a bright side somewhere." There's a bright side somewhere, prophet, don't you rest until you find it. There's a bright side somewhere![51]

Like the prophet Jonah, we too can accept unexpected calls to unexpected places knowing that the will of God will never takes us where the grace of God can't keep us.

FOR REFLECTION

1. Do you agree with Dr. Croft's assertion that the place of prophetic preaching in the African-American church has diminished? Why or why not?

_____

_____

_____

_____

_____

2. What potential benefits for the Church do you see in the postmodern shift that Dr. Croft describes? What are some possible dangers in the postmodern way of thinking that the Church should seek to avoid?

_____

_____

_____

3. Dr. Croft sees Jonah as a prophet for our times, precisely because he wrestled with doubt about God's call (see pg. 19). How have you struggled with God's call on your life?

_____

_____

_____

4. Dr. Croft says Jonah's problems are our problems (see pg. 25). What does he mean? What part can each of us play to eradicate the problems?

_____

_____

_____

_____

Chapter Two

CAN SOMEONE ELSE GO?
JONAH 1:1-2

Now the word of the LORD came to Jonah son of Amittai, saying, "Go at once to Nineveh, that great city, and cry out against it; for their wickedness has come up before me."

The following story is told in a 1993 issue of *Christianity Today*:

"Alila stood on the beach holding her tiny infant son close to her heart. Tears welled in her eyes as she began slowly walking toward the river's edge. She stepped into the water, silently making her way out until she was waist deep, the water gently lapping at the sleeping baby's feet. She stood there for a long time holding the child tightly as she stared out across the river. Then all of a sudden in one quick movement she threw the six month old baby to his watery death.

"Native missionary M. V. Varghese often witnesses among the crowds who gather at the Ganges. It was he who came upon Alila that day kneeling in the sand crying uncontrollably and beating her breast. With compassion he knelt down next to her and asked her what was wrong.

"Through her sobs she told him, 'The problems in my home are too many and my sins are heavy on my heart, so I offered the best I have to the goddess Ganges, my first born son.'

"Brother Varghese's heart ached for the desperate woman. As she wept he gently began to tell her about the love of Jesus and that through Him her sins could be forgiven.

"She looked at him strangely. 'I have never heard that before,' she replied through her tears. 'Why couldn't you have come thirty minutes earlier? If you did, my child would not have had to die.'

"Each year millions of people come to the holy Indian city of Hardwar to bathe in the River Ganges. These multitudes come believing this ritual will wash their sins away. For many people like Alila, missionaries are arriving too late, simply because there aren't enough of these faithful brothers and sisters on the mission field."[52]

The prophet Jonah was being sent to a city that was lost in her sin: the city of Nineveh. Nineveh doesn't realize that it needs Jonah's message of God's redemptive grace in order to survive. If Jonah goes now, Nineveh has a chance of experiencing grace and mercy. But if Jonah had waited any longer someone may have had a question similar to Alila's, "Why couldn't you have come thirty minutes earlier? If you had, we would not have had to die." Jonah, however, does not possess the urgency or concern that one who is called by God should have when they see a city headed for destruction. When God calls Jonah to go and preach repentance to the wicked city of Nineveh, Jonah heads in the opposite direction. With a calling on his life, one would think Jonah, the revivalist, would accept the opportunity. Instead, Jonah is willing to let God send someone else to preach to the people of Nineveh. In fact, Jonah's response is in stark contrast to that of the prophet Isaiah. God asked, "Whom shall I send, and who will go for us?" Isaiah responded, "Here am I; send me!" (Isa. 6:8).

Many of us are like Jonah, in that we don't want to go to Nineveh. We don't want to go to Nineveh because Nineveh has too many challenges. Think about it this way. For many of us Nineveh is not a city. Our Nineveh might be reconciliation with someone who has hurt us, forgiveness for someone who has wronged us, or love for someone who mistreated us in the past and who now longs for our forgiveness. Our Nineveh might be within us. It might be releasing ourselves of the guilt we feel over something we've done in the past that God has already forgiven us of. The Nineveh to which God calls us might be repentance of some damaging habit we have. Our Nineveh might be restitution. But while God is telling us to go to our Nineveh, we willingly disobey and head in another direction! Can someone else go? No! Somewhere there is a job for you that no one else can do quite the way you can. God calls you to do it even though it looks impossible. God knows that you can do it with His help. The reason God will not send anyone else but you is because His calling is personal.

The call to Jonah, likewise, was a personal call. It was "to Jonah" (v. 1). God did not call Habakkuk, Amos, Joel, Obadiah, nor any of the other prophets to go to Nineveh. It was a personal call to Jonah. I don't know how God talked to Jonah. Jonah did not have the written Word of God as we have it now. Neither did Jonah have a commentary to read to find out how God speaks. The text says, "Now the word of the LORD came to Jonah…." (1:1).

Perhaps God spoke to him audibly, as He did with Moses.

Perhaps God spoke to him through His Spirit, as He did with Isaiah.

Perhaps God spoke to him through symbolic language, as He did with Daniel.

Perhaps God spoke to him in a vision, as He did with Ezekiel.

Perhaps God spoke to him in a still small voice, as He did with Elijah.

Perhaps God spoke to him in a dream, as He did with Joseph and Pilate's wife.

But it's not how God spoke to Jonah that's important. What's important is the word of the Lord got through to a human being. God does not mind talking to dust. Our God continues to speak to us today, and the call He makes remains personal. I believe that God speaks to us most clearly through His Word, the Bible. It's a lamp to our feet, a light unto our path, and a plumb line to measure everything by. But God is not limited in His speaking. God can speak to us in ways and places we often overlook. He doesn't always speak in the way that we expect Him to. This is one of the reasons why we often miss God speaking and fail to realize that we have already heard from Him. If we listen and look, God can speak to us through circumstances, crises, disappointments, songs, meditation, the Holy Spirit, nature, etc. God can speak in a combination of different ways, creating a symphony that we begin to hear once we discover how to tune in to God's voice. The good news is we have a God who speaks to our heart, giving us a word that will bring new life. Singer Donnie McClurkin proclaims that God will chase away the darkness if God speaks to our hearts.

God still speaks calling particular people to particular places for particular purposes. The call of the Lord to Jonah—as it is for us—was not only personal but came with direction. I agree with Harold A. Carter who said, "God never calls a person without giving that person a specific assignment, a place to carry out the assignment, and the amazing grace with which to complete the mission."[53]

- When God called Abraham, God told him to leave Haran. The assignment was to walk with Him and he would become the father of nations.
- When God called Moses, God told him to go to Egypt. The assignment was to tell the pharaoh, "Let My people go."
- When God called Joshua, God told him that there was a land flowing with milk and honey. The assignment was to go to Canaan and take possession of that land.
- When God called Ezekiel, God told him to go to a valley full of dry bones. The assignment was to preach the Word of the Lord to those dry bones that they might live.
- When God called Mary, the mother of Jesus, God sent the angel Gabriel to tell her that she was highly favored and was with child. The assignment was to go to Bethlehem and to give birth to our Christ.
- And, when God called Jesus, God sent Him up a hill called Calvary. The assignment was to die on that hill and to save God's people from their sins.

A vast number of people in the history of Israel did not accept God's calling and assignment willingly and right away.

We are the same way. What is your excuse for not responding to God's calling on your life? God does not call us because we are perfect, ready, or equipped. In fact, God doesn't call the equipped; He equips the called. When God calls us for an assignment, God already knows that we are in agony with complaints, low self-esteem, excuses, and difficult emotions. God knows that our lives are like a fragile vessel made of clay, but God also sees the excellency of His power in us. He calls us to a specific vocation. Where is God calling you? To what task is He calling you? Wherever it is, go knowing that God does His perfect work with imperfect instruments.

God called Jonah and said, "Go at once to Nineveh" (1:2). God did not tell him to go to Jerusalem, Joppa, Bethlehem, or Shechem. His call was to Nineveh. Nineveh, however, was not an ideal destination. It was not listed in *Travel Guide.* It was not a city to which one wanted to move, settle, or raise a family. Nineveh was not even on Jonah's preaching itinerary. You see, even though God calls us, it may be that we do not like where God is sending us. The strange place God is sending us, however, may be the place God can use us the best and no one else can go there but us.

God does not simply tell Jonah to go to Nineveh. God said, "Go to Nineveh, that great city" (ibid.). Nineveh was considered great for a number of reasons. First, Nineveh was important because of its location, at the intersection of two important rivers and two important trade routes. Nineveh was also important because, as the capital of the Assyrian Empire, it had a massive population. We know from the last verse of this book (see 4:11) that there were more than 175,000 people living in Nineveh. It must have been the "bright lights, swimming pools, movie stars, and black gold, oil that is, Texas tea" in Nineveh that attracted so many people.

But that's not all, Nineveh was also considered great because it boasted great architecture. Nineveh had beautiful palaces as well as other public buildings. With the inner and outer doors shut, its gateways were virtual fortresses. The bases of its walls and the interior chambers of its gateways were lined with finely cut stone. Truly, Nineveh was great because of its architecture.

Lastly, Nineveh was great because of its learning. Nineveh's library was famous because it possessed more than sixteen thousand clay tablets. If one wanted to do research, Nineveh was the place. But, all of Nineveh's greatness became insignificant when compared to its lack of spiritual awareness. Nineveh was great in the eyes of humankind but not in the eyes of the omniscient God. All of Nineveh's material greatness was no substitute for its spiritual neediness. God is much more concerned about our spiritual state than our worldly standing. The city that the world would call great, God saw to be a total failure.

By the days of the Greek historian Herodotus (ca. 450 B.C.), Nineveh was already a thing of the past; and when Xenophon the historian passed by the place on his march out of Persia (ca. 401 B.C.), the very memory of its name had been lost. It was buried out of sight. Jesus asked the question, "For what will it profit them to gain the whole world and forfeit their life?" (Mark 8:36). In spite of its greatness, Nineveh had an even greater spiritual need. God called the prophet Jonah to go and preach and cry out to Nineveh because of its wickedness. But there was a problem. Most Jews, including Jonah, had it in their minds that God loved them and them alone. When God called Jonah into the ministry, Jonah was excited. But when God told him that his next preaching assignment was in Nineveh, Jonah refused to go. You and I don't get to choose where we will to go and do ministry—that's God's sovereign choice. But Jonah did not want to go to Nineveh, a wicked pagan city. So Jonah said in essence, "Here am I, Lord. But can you send someone else to Nineveh?"

God's call on our lives is not only personal and directed but it also always has a purpose. The word of the Lord came to Jonah from God. That's personal. The place Jonah was to go preach—Nineveh—was assigned by God. That's directed. The reason why Jonah was to preach was given by God. That's purpose. You see, Nineveh had become a wicked and sinful city. Warning the Ninevites of their sin would wake them up to their need for repentance, which would open the door for them to escape from deserved judgment. Nineveh did not deserve the warning, but grace prevailed and Jonah was being sent to preach repentance.

However, it was this knowledge of grace that was at the bottom of Jonah's reluctance to go to Nineveh. Nineveh was Israel's enemy and a threat to Israel's very existence as a nation. Jonah did not want them to experience the grace Israel had experienced. He wanted them to be destroyed. He wanted them to be annihilated. When the call came to go to Nineveh, Jonah knew well the nature of the call. He knew that it sprung from God's grace. But because of his selfish spirit, he refused to go. He was like those who want to take the easy road, catering to the well-to-do and affluent, avoiding people not of their own color, or the downtrodden.

Don't be too quick to throw stones at Jonah because all too often we feel and act like Jonah. We like grace when it benefits us. However, to witness our enemies experiencing grace is another story. We will serve with gladness when our service benefits us or our friends, but we might have a different attitude when our service has the potential to help those who mistreat us. When we read that God called Jonah to go to Nineveh, it should remind us of our commission to go to the ends of the world—which may include those whom we do not like—and tell them about God's love, mercy, and grace.

Jonah's call had purpose: "Go at once to Nineveh, that great city, and cry out against it; for their wickedness has come up before me" (1:2). Jonah was to proclaim to Nineveh that their wickedness had become known to God and that they faced His judgment if they did not repent. But to go to Nineveh to share God's message would be like walking into the middle of the enemy's camp. What a task God assigned him! Jonah would be one lonely voice in the midst of a wicked city, calling its people to revival and repentance. Think about that. What could one man do? Well, when God calls us and sends us, He empowers us with everything we need in order to get the job done. If God sends you, He will give you everything you need to accomplish His will. Far too often, we focus on ourselves. When we see ourselves and our weaknesses, hatred, bitterness, prejudice, anger, low self-esteem, faults, and failures, we want to know if someone else can go in our place. But let me assure you that the God who knows the number of hairs on your head and who has numbered the stars knew your weakness when He called you.

Jonah did not want to go to Nineveh not only because he was prejudiced and Nineveh was considered to be the enemy, but because Jonah believed that Nineveh deserved punishment and not grace for its sin. But, if that was the case, Jonah didn't deserve grace either. What's more, God should not have sent Jesus, who was full of grace and truth (see John 1:16-17), to save you and me. The reason you and I have to go to the Ninevehs in our lives, and cannot send anyone else, is because when we didn't deserve grace God demonstrated His love toward us in sending His Son. As Paul says, "While we were yet sinners, Christ died for us" (Rom. 5:8, KJV). I don't know about you, but when I think about where the Lord has brought me from and how He has showered me with His grace, I would have to go to Nineveh. As I think about it, it was "Amazing grace! How sweet the sound that saved a wretch like me! I once was lost, but now am found; was blind, but now I see." I would have to go and help somebody headed for destruction, who has been marginalized by society, who feels the effects of sexism, classism, and racism, whose life is being torn to shreds, who has a habit they can't break, a sin they can't shake, who keeps making the same mistake, whose relationship is falling apart, and whose marriage is failing or has ended. All because the same grace that saved me is still available. So, Lord, You don't have to send someone else. I'm your prophet, and I'll go where You want me to go. I'll do what You want me to do, and I'll say what You want me to say even if it will cost me my life. Because You sent Your Son to Calvary for me, because He bled for me, because He died for me, was buried for me, got up from the grave for me, He is sitting at the right hand of the Father for me, and because one day He is going to break through the clouds and come back for me, You don't have to send someone else to go and do a work You called me to do. I'll go, I'll go, I'll go, and tell the world about Your amazing grace!

FOR REFLECTION

1. God tells Jonah to "go to the city of Nineveh and preach against it" (1:2). What does this say about God and what He requires of people?

_____

_____

2. Like Jonah, we have received a calling that is specific to our individual abilities or needs. What has God called you to do? How will you go about fulfilling your calling?

_____

_____

_____

3. God's calling to Jonah came to him through a spoken word. Dr. Croft says it's not important how God spoke to Jonah. The important feature of this encounter is that God spoke to a mere person. How does God personally speak to you? To what extent are you confident that you are hearing from God?

_____

_____

4. Recall some of the things God has called you to do in the past? Where are you in fulfilling these requests from God? How will you complete the tasks that are unfinished?

_____

_____

_____

5. Have you ever refused a calling because you did not feel equipped? How has this message helped you to move forward to fulfill God's calling in spite of this deficiency?

_____

_____

_____

6. Dr. Croft says God's calling on our lives is personal (just for you), directed (has a specific target), and purposeful (has a reason). What do each of these elements say about God's relationship with you?

_____

_____

7. This message reveals God's desire to intervene in the lives of people for salvation. Why do you think He does not do this more often?

_____

_____

_____

Chapter Three

WHICH WAY IS UP?
JONAH 1:3

But Jonah set out to flee to Tarshish from the presence of the Lord. He went down to Joppa and found a ship going to Tarshish; so he paid his fare and went on board, to go with them to Tarshish, away from the presence of the Lord.

I am convinced that the book of Jonah is for all of us who have made bad decisions. It's for all of us who have blown it at some point in our lives, whether we have blown it in a way that cost us something of value or through some "small" indiscretion that cost us our integrity. We have all wished, at some point in our lives, that we could re-live some of our past days and undo certain mistakes we have made. The book of Jonah is not simply about a man in a fish. More so, it is about a God who is bigger than the mistakes we have made.

The first two verses of the book say, "Now the word of the Lord came to Jonah son of Amittai, saying, 'Go at once to Nineveh, that great city, and cry out against it; for their wickedness has come up before me.'" God honored Jonah by calling him. I don't know how God called or spoke to Jonah. It may have been in a dream, in a vision, or audibly, but God spoke to him and called him and that's an honor. Out of everyone else, God chose Jonah to go to Nineveh and bring a message of repentance and revival so that they might receive God's grace and mercy. Jonah should have felt privileged to be called by God to carry out such a mission. However, verse three begins with one of the saddest words. The sad word in this verse is the word *but*. Instead of fulfilling the call on his life and the will of God, Jonah went in another direction.

Why? Well, the problem was with where God was calling him to go: Nineveh. Jonah did not want Nineveh to experience the grace that he and others experienced. He felt that because of Nineveh's wickedness, they deserved judgment. Perhaps Jonah also felt some sense of inadequacy because he was one man called to stand before thousands and to urge them to repent. That alone was doubtless intimidating. But Jonah's resistance to going to Nineveh may also have been a result of his own weaknesses and sin. The good news, however, is that before God called Jonah, He already knew Jonah's thoughts, weaknesses, and sins. The beauty of the call is that God called and sent Jonah in spite of his faults. "But" Jonah went in another direction. The text tells us that Jonah fled from the presence of the Lord by going down to Joppa and boarding a ship to Tarshish.

Jonah's flight to Tarshish in the face of a call to Nineveh informs us of the distance Jonah wanted to put between himself and God. Tarshish was the farthest possible (known) distance from Nineveh. It is believed to have been in Spain, more than two thousand miles from Joppa. Tarshish was as far west as one could go. In the mind of an ancient Israelite, going to Tarshish meant going to the farthest point in the world. Jonah, however, will learn that he could never go so far west or east that God could not find him. The author, scholar, and apologist, C. S. Lewis, tells of a young agnostic graduate student at Oxford, Sheldon Vanauken, who had heard of him (i.e., Lewis) and began corresponding with him. As this student posed his doubts and questions to Lewis, Lewis responded very simply, "I think you are already in the meshes of the net! The Holy Spirit is after you. I doubt if you'll get away." Not long afterward, Vanauken, having been pursued by God for so long, finally surrendered. He learned—like Jonah would learn—that when we try to run from God, God has a way of catching up with us. We may run, but God has a way of finding us even when we run to a far-away city like Tarshish.

A lot of us have a Tarshish somewhere, a place we have gone so we would not have to face our Nineveh. The text says Jonah went to flee from the presence of the Lord. In one sense, it is impossible to get away from God's presence simply because He is omnipresent. David understood this truth when he asked, "Where can I go from your spirit? or where can I flee from your presence? If I ascend to heaven, you are there; If I make my bed in hell, behold, you are there. If I take the wings of the morning and settle at the farthest limits of the sea, even there your hand shall lead me, and your right hand shall hold me fast" (Ps. 139:7-10). So again, in one sense, it is impossible to get away from the presence of the Lord.

But the presence of the Lord as used here is not a reference to God's omnipresence. Genesis 4:16 speaks of Cain going "away from the presence of the LORD" after he killed his brother Abel and was rebuked by God. Cain did not escape the omnipresence of God, but rather the particular place where he spoke with God. Similarly, God told disobedient Israel, "Therefore, I will surely lift you up and cast you away from my presence, you and the city that I gave to you and your ancestors" (Jer. 23:39). This did not mean that God was not omnipresent. What it meant was that Israel was going to be separated from some of its spiritual privileges. The temple would be destroyed, and God would stop sending His prophets to Israel to declare His Word. The presence of the Lord, thus, does not always refer to His omnipresence but often to the place where we worship or where we hear God speak. This is why David cried in the midst of his sin, "Do not cast me away from your presence, and do not take your holy spirit from me" (Ps. 51:11). David needed to worship as well as hear God's voice in order to have peace in his life.

Jonah, unfortunately, thought he could flee from God's calling on his life. He should have known better. Jonah's story, though, teaches us that sin has a way of blinding us to the truth. The truth is that none of us can flee from God's presence or get away from Him. But Satan stands ready to convince us that we can do just that. Isn't it interesting that the Bible says Jonah "found a ship" (v. 3). The enemy gave Jonah what He needed in order to avoid doing the will of God. Satan will always make sure that transportation is provided for those who are running from the will of God. Jonah probably thought it couldn't get any better than this! A means of escape lay right in front of him. But we must be most careful exactly when things seem to be falling in place. Just because we "found a ship," doesn't mean it is the right choice.

Don't be fooled. Whenever God calls us and tells us to go to Nineveh, there will always be ships lining up to take us to Tarshish.

Jonah's willing disobedience came with a cost. Disobedience is never free; it costs plenty. Jonah was not exempt from the costs and so "he paid his fare" (ibid.). He would pay the fare to Tarshish in more ways than he realized. The initial cost was not as expensive as what he would pay in the end. His disobedience would eventually cost him his peace of mind, his good conscience, his honor before men, and it almost cost him his life. As Alexander Whyte noted, "No booking clerk could have told Jonah what it was actually going to cost him to get on board."[54] Running away from God is always a costly business. Sometimes when you look at Nineveh and its harsh realities, Tarshish appears to be more attractive. But we often fail to realize that Tarshish is more costly because we go there without God's blessings, and whenever we go anywhere without God's blessing, it costs us.

Furthermore, notice Jonah's downward spiral. "He went down to Joppa" (v. 3, NIV). From there, he went down to the ship, down to Tarshish, and further down as the story progresses. Jonah is a vivid picture of what happens when one tries to flee from God. The only way we can go is down. O. S. Hawkins tells the story of how he and a friend went to learn how to ski: "On the first day of my first attempt, a friend and I got on the wrong ski lift and went to the top of the mountain instead of to the beginners' slope. The farther down we went, the steeper it got and the faster we went and we couldn't stop until we crashed. This is the way it is in leaving the will of God. When we fall from His will it is not only a calculated fall, but a continuous fall until we crash. If we could only learn this simple lesson: No one ever goes up while living in rebellion against God. A lot of people today are fooling themselves. A fall is just what it says it is. People never fall up; they fall down. There is no standing still on the way to Tarshish."[55] But, the good news is if you allow it, grace will break your fall, so you don't have to crash.

There's something else here that I need to tell you. I don't believe Jonah heard God's call, said no, and then started his downward spiral. Jonah's fall started way before he was called to go to Nineveh. It started with something little that Jonah thought would not affect him later in his walk. You see, one sin leads to another. Each sin breaks another fiber of resistance to evil; each fall brings more disabling injury and weakness. It starts with the first drink, the first snort, the first lie. It begins with skipping worship once and soon realizing that what you decide to do "once" has become a habit. Sow a thought; reap an action. Sow an action; reap a character. Sow a character; reap a destiny.

The text says Jonah "went on board, to go with them to Tarshish from the presence of the LORD" (v. 3). While going down to Tarshish, Jonah, no doubt, met some folks that were going down to Tarshish as well. I would imagine that there were some disobedient people on the boat as well, for we can always find a crowd that is "going down" to keep us company. Lot was more comfortable with the unrighteous people of Sodom than he was with godly Abraham. Hobab was more comfortable with nomads than with godly Moses (see Num. 10:29-32). Ahab was more comfortable around wicked Jezebel than he around the prophet Elijah. Sin always finds us a crowd to keep us company while we are on a downward spiral. Sin will push us and bend us in order to break us so that we end up on our backs or in a hole asking, "Which way is up?" Sin blinds our eyes, enflames our passions, removes our joy, scars our soul, stains our lips, tarnishes our testimony, eliminates our victory, and ruins our lives. And sin won't stop until

...every thought we have is corrupt.

...every desire we have is damaging.

...every move we make is ungodly.

...every step we take is wicked.

...everything we touch is defiled.

Furthermore, it will find a crowd to keep you company until you believe right is wrong and wrong is right, leaving you to ask, "How did I get here?" and "Which way is up?"

Jonah is about to realize that fleeing from God's will and call is costly. Ask the Christian that married a non-believer. Ask the addict that picked up a habit that has cost them a good relationship with their family and friends. Ask the lady who sells her body and, though in her twenties, looks forty. Ask the person who gave up their integrity to get a job. Ask the brother in prison who took someone else's life. They are shadows of what they might have been had they asked the right person, "Which way is up?" The most expensive thing a person can do is run from God. It can cost you your family, your job, your reputation, your joy, your peace, and your mind.

The good news is that we don't have to pay the price for sin because Jesus paid our fare on Calvary. You don't have to go down to Tarshish because Christ went to the cross for you. There the Sinless One became sin for the sinner so that the sinner may appear before the throne of God sinless. He died our death so that we might live His life. You don't have to go down in life because "Jesus paid it all, all to Him I owe; Sin had left a crimson stain, He washed it white as snow." Yes, we've all took some wrong turns in life, made some bad decisions and went down some wrong roads. But we found out, often the hard way, which way is up. And the way to get up after you've gone down to Tarshish is up to Calvary.

In the words of a beautiful old hymn: "Alas! and did my Savior bleed and did my Sovereign die! Would He devote that sacred head for such a worm as I? Was it for crimes that I had done He groaned upon the tree? Amazing pity! grace unknown! And love beyond degree! But drops of grief can ne'er repay the debt of love I owe: Here, Lord, I give myself away, 'tis all that I can do. At the cross, at the cross where I first saw the light, and the burden of my heart rolled away. It was there by faith I received my sight, and now I am happy all the day!"[56]

FOR REFLECTION

1. Describe a time in your life when you, like Jonah, did not know which way was up. How did you come through that experience?

_____

_____

2. Dr. Croft hones in on the idea that Jonah "found a ship" (v. 3). What are some of the ships that have presented themselves to you in your own life?

_____

_____

Chapter Four

CAN YOU HEAR ME NOW?
JONAH 1:4-9

But the LORD hurled a great wind upon the sea, and such a mighty storm came upon the sea that the ship threatened to break up. Then the mariners were afraid, and each cried to his god. They threw the cargo that was in the ship into the sea, to lighten it for them. Jonah, meanwhile, had gone down into the hold of the ship and had lain down, and was fast asleep. The captain came and said to him, "What are you doing sound asleep? Get up, call on your god! Perhaps the god will spare us a thought so that we do not perish."

The sailors said to one another, "Come, let us cast lots, so that we may know on whose account this calamity has come upon us." So they cast lots, and the lot fell on Jonah. Then they said to him, "Tell us why this calamity has come upon us. What is your occupation? Where do you come from? What is your country? And of what people are you?" "I am a Hebrew," he replied. "I worship the LORD, the God of heaven, who made the sea and the dry land."

*T*hose who argue that the Bible is an uninterest-ing book have never read the book of Jonah. From beginning to end, this book of forty-eight verses is filled with drama, excitement, suspense, and unusual action. There is never a dull moment in the pilgrimage of Jonah. We encounter more drama as we begin at the fourth verse of the first chapter. Here, Jonah is about to pay the cost for refusing to follow God's command. We often talk about what it costs to *serve* God, but Jonah gives us a vivid picture of what it costs to *leave* God. Jonah, as we know, had a calling on his life and received a call from God to go to Nineveh. He was a prophet of God who knew where God wanted him to go but went in another direction because of where God was sending him. To some degree, Jonah, like Jeremiah, handed God his resignation, refusing to speak for God at the place where God wanted him to speak. Also, Jonah became a dis-obedient prophet who was going contrary to God's direction.

In writing about the Battle of Waterloo, Victor Hugo asked, "Was it possible for Napoleon to win the battle? We answer in the negative. Why? On account of [British gen-eral] Wellington? On account of [Prussian general] Blücher? No; on account of God." Hugo said, "Napoleon had been impeached before the Infinite, and his fall was decreed. He vexed God."[57] Likewise, Jonah upset God by going in an-other direction and thus being disobedient. No matter what he did from here on out, he couldn't win. You see, whenever we go against God, we lose because our arms are too short to box against the hands of God. It's a tragedy to think we can escape the will of God and still win in what we call the game of life. What we end up learning is life outside of God's will is not a game.

God's reaction to Jonah's disobedience was not lacking in love and grace. Yes, God was highly upset with Jonah's disobedience, but His anger was not the last word. In His anger, God was endeavoring in love and mercy to bring Jonah back to the path of obedience. When we forsake God, He does not forsake us. Rather in love and mercy, He sets out to regain and save us from total loss. So when Jonah went another direction, God went after him. Aren't you glad that in our waywardness, God comes after us and never gives up on us? Yes, God pursues us, never gives up on us, and He has the last word on our situation. In verse three it says, "But Jonah," but in verse four it says, "But the LORD." God has something to say when we are disobedient. The text says, "But the LORD hurled a great wind upon the sea, and such a mighty storm came upon the sea…." It does not simply say there "arose" a great wind, but rather, "the LORD hurled a great wind."

God sent the storm in order to capture Jonah's attention. God was trying to keep Jonah from getting deeper into trouble. This is an important lesson. God does not sit idly watching His children head for a fall. Let me serve notice to you. God will do whatever He needs to do to get us back on the path of obedience and to make sure we have the opportunity to break our fall. Sometimes God may have to send a storm to get us out of a boat that's headed for a fall. Let me be clear: the storms that come in our lives are not always from the devil. God sends storms of correction like He did with Jonah and storms of perfection like He did with Job and the Disciples. Sometimes storms come because of our distance from the Lord, but there are others that Satan will send, because we are too close to the Lord. The Lord sent this storm to get Jonah's attention. God was asking, "Jonah, can you hear me now?

Through your actions, I heard what you have to say, Jonah, but through this storm, you can hear what I have to say."

You see, when we go contrary to God's will, He has the capability to send a storm, not intended to push us away from Him but to draw us closer to Him. The Lord sent this storm, and the storm does not only demonstrate God's displeasure with Jonah, but it also demonstrates His love. How does it demonstrate His love? God could have let Jonah crash on life's roller coaster, but God sent a storm to halt Jonah's demise. He will eventually send a fish to protect Jonah while he's on the run. So, not only will Nineveh experience the grace of God, Jonah will also be a recipient of that grace. As the narrative continues, we see that everything and everyone was disturbed by Jonah's disobedience. "But the LORD hurled a great wind upon the sea, and such a mighty storm came upon the sea that the ship threatened to break up. Then the mariners were afraid, and each cried to his god" (vv. 4-5). God was disturbed, the sea was disturbed, and the sailors on the ship were disturbed. Disobedience and sin disturb everything around us. But while everything and everyone were disturbed, Jonah was below deck, sleeping. Jonah had grown so distant from God that he couldn't hear God speaking in the storm. He was content with his rebellion. You see as long as our hearts are broken over sin, as long as it keeps us awake at night, there is still hope. But when we become insensitive to and comfortable in our sin, there's a problem.

The Shawshank Redemption is a movie centered on the lives of two men who, through trials and temptations, survived year after year in a penitentiary in Maine. When they received news of a friend who had committed suicide after being released from prison, one of the characters, known as

"Red," perhaps the wisest and most seasoned of the inmates, explained what happens when people live inside the prison walls too long: "These walls are kind of funny. First you hate them and then you get used to them. Enough time passes and you depend on them." I wonder if this is what happened to Jonah. Did Jonah become so comfortable being outside the will of God that he could sleep while God was attempting to get his attention? When God asked, through a storm, "Can you hear me now?" Jonah did not respond.

We can't point our own fingers at Jonah. As Christians, we too have slept through some storms. We have allowed certain things to occur that would not have occurred had we not been sleeping when they occurred:

While Africans were unwillingly brought here on ships and enslaved, we slept.

While the doctrine of "separate but equal" was allowed to justify systems of segregation, we slept.

While the Supreme Court banned prayer in public schools, we slept.

While Christmas carols and the use of God's name was prohibited in schools, we slept.

While the courts stripped the Ten Commandments from public school walls, we slept.

When it was declared that crosses in city parks were unconstitutional, we slept.

But God never slumbers, sleeps, or gives up on us; He is always shaking America and saying, "Arise, sleeper! How can you sleep?"

You and I can't afford to sleep during a storm, when God is trying to get our attention. The captain asked Jonah, "How can you sleep? Get up and call on your god" (v. 6, NIV).

They begged Jonah to pray to his God so that they would not perish in the storm. Jonah's prayer did not cause God to end the storm so they began to unload the ship's cargo overboard to ease the load. That didn't work, so they cast lots. Notice they said, "Let us cast lots" (v. 7). This means that everyone on the ship was involved. No one was excluded from being responsible for the storm. Each one of them had to look within themselves. Inspecting Jonah must not preclude or exclude subjecting ourselves to the same inspection for we all have to make sure our delinquent accounts with God are not causing storms in our lives.

The text says they cast lots to discover which person on board the ship was the cause of the storm. Some people may disapprove of the system these sailors used to detect the culprit because they see it as a form of gambling. The system, however, does not justify gambling of any kind. The fact that God used the casting of lots to expose Jonah does not justify evil anymore than God using the wrath of man to praise Him (see Ps. 76:10) justifies the unholy wrath of man. It simply demonstrates the fact that God controls all things as He wills. There were occasions in the Bible in which the lot was used with divine sanction. But for the most part, the casting of lots has not been associated with divine approval and honor.

It was used to determine which of two goats would be the scapegoat on the Day of Atonement (see Lev. 16:6-10).

It was used to expose Achan (see Josh. 7:14).

It was used in dividing up the land of Canaan among the tribes of Israel (see Josh. 18:6).

It was used to choose the cities in which the sons of Aaron were to live (see 1 Chron. 6:54).

It was used to determine the various duties of the priests, the singers, and other personnel in the tabernacle (see 1 Chron. 25-26).

It was used to see which of two men, Barsabbas or Matthias, would replace Judas (see Acts 1:26).

It was used at the foot of the cross where the soldiers cast lots for the robe of Christ (see Matt. 27:35).

When the casting of lots was done with divine approval it was done to discern the will of God. However, we don't need to cast lots to determine God's will. We have God's Word that gives us the principles necessary to guide our decisions. Also, we have the indwelling of the Holy Spirit that gives us discernment. Why cast lots when we can profit from God's Word? His Word is a lamp unto your feet and a light unto your path (see Ps. 119:105).

When those sailors cast their lots, the lot fell on Jonah. Jonah illustrates that when we are on the run from God, we may be able to hide for a little while (or think we are hiding), but sooner or later, we will be found out. Jonah learned that the Bible is right when it says: "Be sure your sin will find you out" (Num. 32:23). The sailors said five important things to Jonah in verse eight:

"Tell us why this calamity has come upon us."

"What is your occupation?"

"Where do you come from?"

"What is your country?"

"And of what people are you?"

God, however, only wanted to know the answer to one question, "Jonah, can you hear me now?" But all Jonah could do was reply to the sailors saying, "I am a Hebrew ... I worship the LORD, the God of heaven, who made the sea and the dry land" (v. 9). Jonah realized he couldn't get away from God because he belonged to God. Furthermore, because God made the sea that he was presently on and the land he was previously on, there was no hiding or escaping from God.

The truth is that most of us do not want to face our Nineveh—those harsh and unattractive places in our lives. So we find a ship and get on board to flee from God. But then, we find out that God is not a delinquent parent. God chases us down by way of a storm. For some of us, it feels like everything is falling apart, and the more we try to flee from God, rather than to God, the unhappier we become. But thank God for the storm that woke some of us up. For if God had not sent the storm when He sent it, some of us would still be sleeping in disobedience. Although we thought the storm was going to kill us—and it just might have if we hadn't arose—it really was God's grace and mercy trying to save us from our own demise. God could have allowed Jonah, and all of us, to die in our rebellion. He could have allowed it to wipe us out, but thank God, the storm is not simply God's way of getting our attention. When the storm is sent to awake—and save us, it becomes to us a sign that says God is not finished with us yet; and when the Lord gets us back on the right path and He gets through using us, we will come forth as pure gold. So I don't know about you, but:

Is there anybody who has a "through it all" praise? Is there anybody who can say, "Since I've been delivered from my storm, I don't want God to have to send another storm my way to get my attention. After all that I've been through, outside His will, I now want to stay in His will." Yes, I can hear Him now. In the words of E. W. Blandy:

I can hear my Savior calling,
I can hear my Savior calling,
I can hear my Savior calling,
"Take thy cross and follow, follow Me."

I'll go with Him thru the garden,
I'll go with Him thru the garden,
I'll go with Him thru the garden,
I'll go with Him, with Him all the way.

I'll go with Him thru the judgment,
I'll go with Him thru the judgment,
I'll go with Him thru the judgment,
I'll go with Him, with Him all the way

He will give me grace and glory,
He will give me grace and glory,
He will give me grace and glory,
And go with me, with me all the way.
Where He leads me I will follow,
Where He leads me I will follow,
Where He leads me I will follow,
I'll go with Him, with Him all the way.[58]

FOR REFLECTION

1. Dr. Croft—through a clever use of the advertising slogan "Can you hear me now?"—points out that God uses catastrophic events as a way of getting our attention. What are instances in your life (or in the lives of friends or family members) that God has used to get your attention?

_____

_____

2. What are some of the practical costs of choosing to flee from God?

_____

_____

3. What is your "Nineveh"? What will it take for you to muster the courage to face it?

_____

_____

4. Jonah tried to escape from God because he did not want to go to Nineveh. What about God makes it impossible to run from Him?

_____

_____

5. When trying to escape from God, how is facing a storm in life different or the same as facing God?

_____

_____

_____

Chapter Five

THE PERFECT STORM
JONAH 1:10-17

"Then the men were even more afraid, and said to him, 'What is this that you have done!' For the men knew that he was fleeing from the presence of the LORD, because he had told them so. Then they said to him, 'What shall we do to you, that the sea may quieten down for us?' For the sea was growing more and more tempestuous. He said to them, 'Pick me up and throw me into the sea; then the sea will quieten down for you; for I know it is because of me that this great storm has come upon you.' Nevertheless, the men rowed hard to bring the ship back to land, but they could not, for the sea grew more and more stormy against them. Then they cried out to the LORD, 'Please, O LORD, we pray, do not let us perish on account of this man's life. Do not make us guilty of innocent blood; for you, O LORD, have done as it pleased you.' So they picked Jonah up and threw him into the sea; and the sea ceased from its raging. Then the men feared the LORD even more, and they offered a sacrifice to the LORD and made vows. But the LORD provided a large fish to swallow up

Jonah; and Jonah was in the belly of the fish for three days and three nights."

No one is immune to the storms of life. Storms come to the best of us. They come to the rich and the poor. They come to males and females. They have no respect for race or status. However, storms are not always bad. A vast number of the great men and women we admire were made great because of the storms they encountered and overcame in life. In fact, most of the great hymns and anthems we love to sing were written out of these storm experiences. Always remember that a person is not remembered by how they act when things are in control, but by how they react when things are out of control. So how should we react to storms? Well, some persons cry through them; some try to avoid them; some weather them; while others allow them to defeat them.

When the prophet Jonah was attempting to flee the presence of God by boarding a ship in Joppa, I am sure he did not expect to leave the ship in the midst of a storm. Jonah learned, however, that the travel agent for disobedience never advertises truthfully. He shows you how nice it is in Tarshish and provides you with beautiful brochures, but he never tells you about the storms that come with traveling to Tarshish outside the will of God. We have to be aware of disobedience's travel agents that speak enthusiastically about Tarshish when God is telling us to go to Nineveh. Jonah expected to walk off the ship in Tarshish, but instead, he was thrown off the ship and into the sea. Even so, it was the perfect storm for someone on the run from God's will.

The text tells us that the sailors asked Jonah, "What shall we do to you, that the sea may quiet down for us?" (v. 11).

They had found the cause of the storm—Jonah—and wanted to do something about it. Like these men, in the midst of our storms, we are often more concerned with identifying the cure than the cause. They didn't care about the cause but only the cure. Often the reason we cannot find the cure is that we have not discovered the cause or have not wanted to deal with the cause. But, in order to quiet the storm, we have to deal with the cause or the storm will keep returning. We must all learn that storms are inevitable, both storms of perfection and storms of correction. Some storms come from God when we are too distant from Him. Other storms come from Satan when we are too close to God. This storm came as a result of Jonah's rebellion against the will of God.

The reason God did not stop the storm after Jonah was asked by the captain to pray is because Jonah was focused on the cure: "throw me into the sea" (v. 12). He did not want to face the cause of the storm. In the midst of crisis, instead of being taken to Nineveh, he settles for being thrown overboard. He would rather die at sea than do the will of God. One can hardly believe how rebellious and stubborn human nature is until we see Jonah. The only thing Jonah had going for him was that God sent the storm. If the enemy had sent the storm, Jonah would have died. Remember that, according to verse 4, God sent the storm. It's safer to be in a storm with God than to be on dry land without Him. Even when I am in a rebellious state and about to be thrown overboard, because I am God's child, I am still safe in the storm. It may not sound like good news, but the good news is that God will send a storm to get our attention. He's not trying to kill us. He's trying to save us. He sends the "perfect storm" to keep us from making an even worse mistake.

Let me go further. What's amazing to me is that even after Jonah had gone to Joppa, found a ship, and headed to Tarshish, God was still willing to use him to bring revival to Nineveh. Too many times we allow our past failures to hinder our future success. We think we've failed, we've messed up, or God can't use us again. The storm may come to us as an indication that God is not through with us yet. If God were through with us, He would not continue to pursue us. God could have let Jonah die in his rebellion. Often the reason and purpose for the storm is that God still wants to use us and that makes it the "perfect storm." Yet when storms come in our lives, we think God is angry with us, or we have sinned and knew deep down that eventually something like this would happen. For example, some say, "Ten years ago, I did X or Y, and this is God's way of getting back at me." Although our wrongdoing can cause storms to erupt in our lives, as it did in Jonah's life, our storms are not always a result of the mistakes we made in the past. We are all recipients of two things: grace and mercy. If God wanted to get back at us for all the mistakes we made in the past, none of us would be here today. The psalmist was correct when he wrote in Psalm 103: "He does not deal with us according to our sins, nor repay us according to our iniquities … As a father has compassion for his children, so the LORD has compassion for those who fear him" (vv. 10, 13).

When we discover the root cause of our storms there are several ways we might react. The reaction of the sailors was to row harder. They did their best to row toward land. In their own strength, they tried to save Jonah. But the story of Jonah illustrates that no one can save you out of your storm. Rather, you have to take responsibility for your storm. The tragedy is, these men put more effort into trying to save Jonah than Jonah did in trying to save Nineveh. They tried hard to get back to safety but quickly learned that it is futile to fight against God's will. Notice that these sailors tried two things before they surrendered to the will of God. First, "they threw the cargo into the sea to lighten the ship" (Jon. 1:5, NIV). They thought that by getting rid of the cargo, they could ride out the storm. We fail in this thinking. We attempt to calm the storms in our lives by getting rid of certain cargo. But God doesn't want the cargo; God wants us. We can give up certain pieces of cargo but still have no peace.

The sailors then cast lots to determine who was responsible for the mess they were in. Now, there was only one way they could be saved: Jonah had to be thrown overboard. But they did not want to face that choice. So according to verse thirteen, they "rowed hard to bring the ship back to land." This did not work, "so they picked Jonah up and threw him into the sea; and the sea ceased from its raging" (v. 15). For many of us in order for the storm to cease in our lives, there are some people and friends that may have to be thrown overboard. They are outside the will of God, and they have become a hindrance to us. "Jonah's got to go." Jonah said, "Pick me up and throw me into the sea, and it will become calm. I know that it is my fault..." (v. 12, NIV). Jonah reacted by accepting the blame. He had stopped running at this point. He admitted his sin and disobedience, took responsibility for it, and submitted himself to God. Jonah had to be sacrificed in order for the sailors to be saved. This is what Christ did for us to save us. He gave His own life so we could live.

Notice, when Jonah was in his rebellious state, the sky was dark, the thunder roared, the lightning flashed, the winds blew, and the waves beat against the ship. But the moment he surrendered to God's will, peace came. Also, notice that the Lord sent the storm (see v. 4), and the Lord prepared a great fish (see v. 17). He sent the storm to get Jonah's attention, but He also prepared a fish to protect him. God can provide for His people in incredible and miraculous ways, and He can use His creatures in the process.

God used ravens to bring Elijah food (see 1 Kings 17).

God used a fish to bring a coin to Peter to pay his taxes (see Matt. 17:24-27).

God used a donkey to speak to the prophet Balaam to tell him some important truths he needed to know (see Num. 22).

God provides us with what we need to take us where He wants us to go, and He provides it in miraculous ways.

Many of us have a Jonah testimony. When our distance and disobedience, our stubbornness and straying, our running away and rejection of God's Word caused us to be thrown overboard and in danger of drowning, the Lord provided a miracle. The Lord gave us just what our own individual situation needed: a way out of no way. When we were in danger of drowning:

- Grace and mercy lifted us up
- Love and forgiveness washed us up
- The blood of Jesus covered us up
- The Holy Spirit cleaned us up
- The promises of God picked us up

For Jonah, being in the belly of the fish was not all that bad in the end. Why do I say this? Well, it was in the belly of the fish that Jonah began to look more like Jesus. Jesus said, "For just as Jonah was three days and three nights in the belly of the sea monster, so for three days and three nights the Son of Man will be in the heart of the earth" (Matt. 12:40). Jonah, in the belly of a fish, looks like Jesus buried in the earth. Everyone does not learn their lesson in the belly of a fish. Moses had to be taught some things on the back side of the desert. Jacob had to learn some things down at his uncle Laban's house. David had to learn some things in the midst of sheep. The three Hebrew boys had to learn some things in a fiery furnace. Daniel had to learn some things in a lion's den. Paul had to learn some things on the Damascus road. What each of these individuals learned could not have been learned any place else. Let me tell you, these are not pretty places to be but each one of them was a place where God shaped His servants.

There is a story told about a couple who loved to visit antique shops. While traveling in England, they visited a shop that stocked all kinds of antique dishes. This was their twenty-fifth wedding anniversary, and on this day in this beautifully adorned shop, they saw an exquisite teacup on the shelf. They asked the owner of the shop, "May we see that teacup? We have never seen one quite so beautiful." The lady behind the counter handed it to them. Quite suddenly, as they received the teacup from the shopowner, it began to speak. It said to her, "Ma'am, I have not always been a teacup. There was a time when I was red clay. One day my master showed up and scooped me out of the ground. He took me home, put me on the table, rolled me, patted me, pushed me, and squeezed me. I yelled out, 'Why don't you leave me alone?' But he just smiled and said, 'Not yet!'

"Then all of a sudden he put me on a spinning wheel and there I was without any control over my circumstances, just spinning around and around and around. I couldn't stop it. I felt dizzy and I screamed, 'Would you stop it?' But the master just shook his head and said, 'Not yet!'

"Then he put me in the oven. I have never felt so much heat. I wondered why anyone would want to torture me like this. I yelled and yelled. I banged on the door of the furnace, for I could see him through the small opening. I could even read his lips as he looked at me. I screamed, 'Let me out! Let me out!' He just smiled and said, 'Not yet.'

"Then all of a sudden the door opened and he put me on the shelf. I began to cool down and relax. I said to myself, 'Now, that's better.' But then he began to paint me all over. The fumes were horrible. I thought I would gag. I said, 'Why are you changing me like this? Stop it! Stop it! Stop it!' But he just smiled and said, 'Not yet.'

"Then he put me back in the oven again. However, it was not like the first oven. This one was twice as hot. I knew that I was done this time I would suffocate. I begged, pleaded, screamed, cried, and the whole time I could see him through the opening just nodding his head and saying, 'Not yet.'

"When I was sure there was no more hope, that I would never make it and was ready to give up, the door opened. He took me out of the oven and set me on the shelf. One hour later, he placed me in front of a mirror and said, 'Now look at yourself.' When I looked at myself I said, 'That couldn't be me. I'm just red clay. I'm not that beautiful.' But then the master spoke to me and said, 'I want you to remember that, while it hurt to be rolled, patted, pushed, and squeezed, if I had left you by yourself where I found you, you would have remained dirt. I know it made you dizzy to spin around on the wheel, but if I had stopped when you asked me, you would have crumbled in my hands. I know it was painful, hot, and uncomfortable when I put you in the oven, but if I hadn't, you would have cracked as soon as I took you out. I know the fumes were bad as I brushed you and painted you, but if I had never done that, you would have never had any color for the rest of your life. And if I hadn't put you back in the oven the second time, you would never have become a finished product. So, after all that you've been through, recognize how the pain has blessed you and made you what you are today.'"

If you're on the spinning wheel or in the oven of life, or you feel like you are in the belly of the fish like Jonah, just "wait for the LORD, be strong, and let your heart take courage" (Ps. 27:14). God will get you back on the right track no matter what it takes because He loves you. He may have to send the perfect storm to do so but that perfect storm is sent to perfect you. And, when the Lord gets through with you, one day you will look in the mirror and see just how beautiful the storm has made you and developed you. That's why it's called the "perfect storm."

FOR REFLECTION

1. What are the root causes of the storms you have faced in life?

_____

_____

2. We may be confronted with storms in life when we disobey

or refuse God's calling. For what other purposes does God allow storms in our lives?

_____

_____

3. What miracle has God used to rescue you from your storm?

_____

_____

_____

4. How have the storms in your life changed your view of and your relationship with God?

_____

_____

_____

5. What do you believe God would have you to do when you are overwhelmed by the storms of life?

_____

_____

_____

Chapter Six

PRAYING YOUR WAY OUT
JONAH 2:1-2

Then Jonah prayed to the LORD his God from the belly of the fish, saying, "I called to the LORD out of my distress, and he answered me; out of the belly of Sheol I cried, and you heard my voice."

*T*he pages of history are filled with stories of men and women who have been down and have made what we call a "comeback." In the field of science, there is Thomas Edison, the great inventor of the light bulb. Before Edison invented it, he failed at more than one hundred other inventions. Someone asked Edison, "Are you a failure for not succeeding in your one hundred other inventions?" Edison replied in essence, "Not only did I make a comeback, but I also succeeded in finding one hundred things that don't work so people won't try them." In the Bible, there are also those who have made some great comebacks, such as Moses who murdered an Egyptian, Elijah who fell into a deep depression, Peter who denied Christ three times, and Jonah who came to be labeled the reluctant prophet. Jonah reminds us that we should not allow our past failures to hinder our future successes. Since God has a plan and purpose for each one of us, God will never give up on us no matter how bad we started off with Him.

You remember how Jonah's preaching pilgrimage began. Jonah was called by God to go to the wicked city of Nineveh to preach repentance. However, Jonah disobeyed God: he went down to Joppa, purchased a ticket, and boarded a ship bound for Tarshish. However, Jonah's ticket cost more than he actually paid. As I stated in the previous chapter, we often talk about what it costs to serve the Lord. Jonah demonstrates in living color what it costs to not serve the Lord. Jonah paid the fare to go to Tarshish. God said, "Nineveh!" Jonah said, "Tarshish!" Thus Jonah boarded a ship to go to Tarshish, but he never made it. Let me ask you a question: Aren't you glad that God didn't let you get to some places you were on your way to in order to get away from Him? If you had arrived, life would have been different, or you might not have been here today. God interrupted Jonah's travel plans by sending a storm, having Jonah thrown overboard by the sailors, and then allowing a large fish to swallow him and protect him while God prepared him for the mission ahead. Because of the bad decisions we've made, God sometimes has to intervene in order to save us from ourselves. We think the holding pattern that God has us in is bad. But if God had allowed us to keep going in the direction we were going, we would be worse off now than we would have ever been. The safest place for us might be the belly of the fish.

I remember being on a flight a few years ago, returning to Philadelphia from Columbus, Ohio. I was in Columbus preaching at the Mount Olivet Baptist Church where my good friend, Rev. Charles E. Booth, serves as pastor. After preaching and having a great meal with Dr. Booth, he took me to the airport, and I boarded my plane. I was tired and could not wait to get home. However, my flight was delayed. We circled in the air for an hour because the pilot said that it was not safe to land. I was frustrated, irritable, and tired. I wanted to get home and get in my bed. However, I realized that the pilot knew what was best. He was trying to save the lives of those of us on the plane and not put us in danger. Once I came to this realization, I further realized that I was safer on the plane circling in the air than I would be had he tried to land. Sometimes God has to place us in a holding pattern for our own good because God knows that if He lets us run on our own, not only will we go further outside His will, but we will also encounter dangers that we are unprepared to handle.

Well, the text says, "Then Jonah prayed..." (v. 1). When is "then"? "Then" is after he had disobeyed God, went contrary to God's direct orders, suffered in a storm, had been thrown overboard, and ended up in the belly of a fish. Then, Jonah prayed. His conduct changed for the better when he was thrown overboard. Jonah had to go through all of this before he finally got on his knees, repented, and said, "Lord, I'll go." I am sure that God would rather us not go through all of the troubles we go through, but God will also do whatever needs to be done to get us on our knees, praying and seeking the right direction. But before we turn our nose up at Jonah, if we are honest with ourselves many of us do the same thing. Just as long as we are able to do something about our situation, we are fine. Just as long as the doctor is able to prescribe medicine for our pain, we are fine. Just as long as the bank is able to help us with our financial needs, we are fine. Just as long as friends are there when we need them, we are fine. Just as long as we have the pleasures of life, we are fine. But there will come a "then" time. We all need to have sincere and fervent talks with God before "then" comes.

The truth is, trouble is not all bad if that trouble leads us back to God. But I would also inform you that you don't have to wait for trouble to find you in order to pray and return to God. In fact, if you pray before trouble comes, when trouble arrives you won't have to look for God, and God won't have to look for you because you and God will have been talking all along the way.

The text further says, "Then Jonah prayed to the LORD his God." Even though he rebelled, Jonah was in a covenant relationship with God. He could pray to the Lord because even though Jonah had forsaken Him, the Lord never forsook Jonah. Some think that because they have broken fellowship with God, they also have a broken relationship with God. It doesn't matter what my children do, they will always be my children. I may have to discipline them, but they are still my children. And as disobedient as Jonah was, as rebellious as he had become, and as much as he had gone in the opposite direction regarding God's will for his life, he still realized that he was God's child. He did not pray to the pagan gods: they couldn't help him. He did not cast lots: they were of no use. He did not pray to Baal: he couldn't deliver him. No. Jonah prayed to the Lord. I don't know about you, but I don't want God to be my last resource. I want God to be my first option. If God is my first option, God will be my only and final option. Some of us have gone our own way. We've resisted the will of God, paid a costly fare, been battered by a storm, and swallowed up into what feels like the belly of a fish. But we've come out learning some valuable lessons in the belly of the fish. We've learned that there's no place we can be where God is not, and even though we may be in a bad situation, God is always there keeping us, providing for us, and protecting us in our suffering.

We now know when and to whom Jonah prayed, but the text also lets us know from where Jonah prayed. The text says, "Then Jonah prayed unto the LORD his God from the belly of the fish." When God is trying to get our attention, He may have to place us in the belly of the fish in order to give us solitude and time with Him. Prayer allows us to reflect on and rejoice over what God has already done. Replaying divine highlights from our walk with God in days past will fortify our prayers. We know what God can do, based upon what God has already done. When our hands are tied, and our situation causes us to feel like we are in the belly of a fish, we have to remember prayerfully how God's hands have moved on our behalf in the past, making a way out of no way, opening and shutting doors, showering us with blessings, defeating our enemies, giving us direction, and delivering us from what appeared to be impossible situations. Prayer in the belly of the fish encourages reflection on what God has done and injects us with faith in what God is able to do. God knows that we will learn more in the belly of a fish then we would on dry land. We can't get a cellular signal in the belly of the fish, which means our cell phone won't ring. We can't receive faxes, emails, tweets, or Facebook messages. There are no friends to help us there. No, the belly of the fish is the place where it's just God and us.

I don't think I am going too far in assuming that in the belly of the fish Jonah tried everything he could to get out on his own. Jonah twisted! Jonah turned! Jonah cried! Jonah squirmed! Jonah pushed! Jonah screamed! But when he recognized that he couldn't get out of the belly of the fish on his own, the text says, "Then Jonah prayed." You see in order to get out of the belly of the fish, we have to pray our way out. The experience can be so bad that prayer is our only option. According to verse two, Jonah felt like he was in hell. He was not just in the belly of a fish praying. Jonah was going through a hellish experience. Hell is not just a place of punishment after one dies or, depending on how it is used, just a derogatory word. If we ignore God, live in disobedience, and disregard God's Word, we can end up creating our own private hell. It also is not only an otherworldly experience. Hell is a fact of this life. For some:

Hell is living through some form of abuse or pain.

Hell is suffering from an ailment you can't shake.

Hell is a situation in which women are physically, emotionally, and mentally abused.

Hell is a man living in a home where he is not respected, cherished, or loved.

Hell is a situation that tortures before it destroys.

Hell is a situation from which there seems to be no exit, no escape, and no end.

But no matter what our experience is and no matter what it feels like, always remember there is a way out. We all need to know that deliverance is a possibility. For when we know that we're not stuck, we can endure the pain, handle the hardship, survive the trial, and get out of the belly of the fish. But we must first pray. Because the only One that can get us out is

God, "a very present help in trouble" (Ps. 46:1). If you are in the belly of the fish and you've had enough, there is a way out and that is to pray your way out. Jonah prayed in the belly of the fish though he felt like he was in a hellish situation. He knew that God could hear him. Maybe Jonah thought like the psalmist: "Where can I go from your spirit? Or where can I flee from your presence? If I ascend to heaven, you are there; if I make my bed in Sheol, you are there. If I take the wings of the morning and settle at the farthest limits of the sea, even there your hand shall lead me, and your right hand shall hold me fast" (Ps. 139:7-10). Jonah could pray after being disobedient, rebellious, contrary, and in the belly of a fish because no matter what, God was with him.

It may seem useless to pray when you're in the belly of a fish. God might even seem to be far away. But keep praying. Jonah said, "I called to the LORD out of my distress, and he answered me; out of the belly of Sheol I cried, and you heard my voice" (v. 2). This was a great comeback. After his failure, Jonah returned to the Lord and cried out to Him, and the Lord heard him. God answered Jonah at the lowest point in his life. God said, "Jonah, where are you?" Jonah said, "I'm on my knees." God said, "That's just where I've been trying to get you."

One day a kindergarten class went on a field trip to a local fire station. After the children had an opportunity to examine the fire trucks, the firefighters' gear and their living quarters, one of the firemen began to talk to them about fire safety. He said, "If you think your house might be on fire, you should not touch the door knob if you are in a room." He asked, "Does anyone know why?" No one raised their hand. He said, "Because you might burn your hand from the heat on the knob." He said, "The second thing is this: if you are in a room, don't open the door." He asked, "Does anyone know why?" No one raised their hand. He said, "Because you will experience a backdraft, and the fire will come into where you are." He continued, "The last and most important thing you need to know in case of a fire: you should get down as low as you can, get on your knees." He asked, "Does anyone know why?" One little boy in the front raised his hand and said, "So we can pray and ask God to get us out of this mess!"

I don't know what your situation is. I don't know what you might be going through, but if you want out, then you have to get on your knees, pray, and ask God to get you out of this mess. And, because God is faithful, He will do it if you let Him. Joseph M. Scriven was correct when he wrote, "O, what peace we often forfeit, O, what needless pain we bear, all because we do not carry everything to God in prayer!"[59]

FOR REFLECTION

1. Describe a time in your life when you made a comeback from a low point or a time of despair. What were some of the factors that enabled that comeback?

_____

_____

2. Do you have to go into the belly of the fish alone? Can someone go with you? Why or why not?

_____

_____

Chapter Seven

THE GOD OF ANOTHER CHANCE, PT. 1
JONAH 3:1-2

The word of the LORD came to Jonah a second time, saying, "Get up, go to Nineveh, that great city, and proclaim to it the message that I tell you."

he Scottish preacher, Alexander Whyte (1836-1921), once said, "The victorious Christian life is a series of new beginnings." He was absolutely correct. It appears that we are always starting over in different areas of our lives. However, the enemy wants us to believe that once we have failed, there is no hope for recovery, bouncing back, or beginning again even though we have repented. God, however, lets us know that He is a God who offers us new beginnings. We don't have to read far into the Bible to discover this truth.

When Abraham fled to Egypt, after he lied about Sarah in order to save his own life, God gave him another chance and he became the father of the faith.

When the patriarch Jacob lied to his father Isaac about who he was, God gave him another chance and used him to build the nation of Israel.

When Moses killed a man and fled Egypt, God gave him another chance by calling him to be the leader of His people.

When Peter denied Christ not once but three times, God gave him another chance and said, "Follow Me." Peter became an effective disciple and preacher.

God is not just a God of second chances, for many of us used our second chance a long time ago. God is the God of another chance. The story of the reluctant prophet Jonah demonstrates this truth very well.

Jonah had previously failed to do what God had called him to do. From a human perspective, it's an open question as to whether, at this point in his life, God would ever use him again. However, God uses people who have failed.

God used Noah, who had a drinking problem.

God used Abraham, Isaac, and Jacob, who all had lied.

God used Sarah, who laughed at Him.

God used Moses, who could not control his anger.

God used Elijah, who suffered with depression.

God used David, who was wanted for murder, lying, and adultery.

God used Peter, who denied Christ.

Theodore Roosevelt once said, "The only man who never makes a mistake is the man who never does anything." The good news is that when we have failed or messed up, the God we serve has a way of taking our failures and turning them into miracles so that others might see how powerful God truly is. He's a God of another chance. I like this first verse, "The word of the LORD came to Jonah a second time...." You will remember that before God spoke to the fish, Jonah said

"But I with the voice of thanksgiving will sacrifice to you; what I have vowed I will pay. Deliverance belongs to the LORD!" (2:9). It's easy to make a promise when we are in a bad situation and our circumstances cause us to feel like our back is up against a wall. We make promises in those types of conditions by saying, "Lord if you get me out of this, I promise to...." But as soon as God delivers us, we end up going back to what we used to do and forget about the promise we made to God. To find out whether Jonah had truly repented, God came to him a second time with the same charge. It appeared by his language in chapter two that Jonah meant business this time. Whether or not he was sincere would be confirmed not by his talk but by how he responded to God's orders the second time.

Notice, God does not change the orders he gave to Jonah in chapter one. Jonah still has to go to Nineveh. After his spiritual temper tantrum, being thrown into the sea and into the belly of a fish, God gives him the same orders, "Arise, go unto Nineveh, that great city" (KJV). I believe in some sense this illustrates that wherever we have failed, there is a good chance we will be tried again for the purpose of examining our repentance. God won't let us get away with failing in an area of our life that He wants us to conquer. If we have failed in a specific area and have repented, our repentance may be examined by another test in that area. We can argue that God does not need to examine us for God knows what is in our hearts without having to examine us. The test, however, is not for God but for us to see whether or not our repentance was genuine. The word comes the second time so that this time we can put our faith and trust in the Examiner who helps us pass every test that comes our way.

God was under no obligation to call Jonah a second time to do what he was supposed to do the first time. The fact that it came the second time is a demonstration of God's grace as well as His mercy. Jonah did not merit a second chance to do what he should have done the first time, but God gave him a second chance. This second chance is also seen in the life and history of Israel. It began with Abraham. God called Abraham the first time when he was in Ur of the Chaldees, but Abraham failed to fulfill the call and stopped in Haran instead of going into the land of Canaan. After some years, Abraham's father, Terah, died and Abraham received a second call. He followed the call and became known as the father of the faith.

The first time God brought Israel to Kadesh-barnea and told them to enter into the Promised Land, the people rebelled. But when God told the next generation, they were ready and they willingly entered the land.

The first time Joseph's brothers came to Egypt to buy food they did not recognize their brother whom they had sold into slavery. But the second time Joseph revealed himself to them and gave them what they needed so they would not die.

The first time God wrote the Commandments on tablets of stone, they were smashed to pieces because of Israel's sin of worshiping the golden calf. The second time, the tablets of stone remained intact and were placed and preserved in the Ark of the Covenant and then written in our hearts.

God is always offering second chances. God would have been justified to reject Jonah and call someone else but grace and mercy was on Jonah's side. This tells us that God had just as much faith in Jonah accomplishing His will with the odds against him as Jonah had in himself with God on his side.

But that's not all! God does not simply see something good in Jonah. God also calls Nineveh great. Four times in this short book, God calls Nineveh great. God, however, knows Nineveh is a wicked city.

The Ninevites were known for their violence.

They showed no mercy to their enemies.

They tortured their victims by leaving them to roast to death in the desert sun.

They beheaded people by the thousands and stacked their skulls up in piles by the city gates.

They skinned their enemies alive.

They respected neither age or sex and killed innocent children so they wouldn't have to take care of them.

Yet God called Nineveh great because God saw what they could become. And the reason God keeps giving us another chance after we've messed up, fallen short, made mistakes, or took a bad turn in life is because God sees us not for what we were and are but for what we can become. All of the storms we went through in life—the feeling of being thrown overboard, the feeling of being in the belly of a fish, the trials we endured and the pain we've encountered—may have come our way to prepare and make us into the person God wants us to be. The reason God keeps calling us and giving us another chance is because He is not through with us.

William Barclay tells the following story: Once someone came upon Michelangelo chipping away with his chisel at a huge shapeless piece of rock. He asked the sculptor what he was doing. "I am releasing the angel imprisoned in this marble," he answered. Could it be that God sees an angel inside of us and is using the storms of life in order to release that angel inside of us? God sees something in you that He can use to His glory and honor. Aren't you glad that God is the God of another chance? Had it been up to us, you and I would be done for. But thanks be to God! We have a God that gives us another, and another, and another chance. Yes at times judgment and rebuke may come when we mess up, but thank God that because we are still alive, we are able to right our wrongs. Truth be told we are all like Jonah. The first time we heard about Christ, we did not heed His call. If He had not given us another chance, we would still be ...

Lost in our sins
Dead in our trespasses
Consumed by His anger
Wretched in our ways
Helpless in our defense
Miserable in our mess
Confused in our thoughts
Troubled in our minds.

But because He is a God of another, and another, and another chance, instead of being all those things and more, we are...

Saved by His grace
Filled with His Spirit
Clothed in His righteousness
Secured in His love
Refreshed through His presence
Assured by His voice
Healed by His touch
Strengthened by His power
Calmed through His peace and washed in His blood.

Yes, because He gave us another chance, we are saved by His power divine and saved to new life sublime. Life now is sweet and our joy is complete for we are saved, saved, saved! Thank God, He's the God of another chance. For it is of the Lord's mercies we are not consumed—Thank God, He is a God of another chance. For as a Father pitieth His children so the Lord pitieth them that fear Him—Thank God, He is the God of another chance. For God commended His love toward us that while we were yet sinners, Christ died for us—Thank God, He is the God of another chance. For what love has the Father bestowed upon us that we should be called the sons and daughters of God—Thank God, He is the God of another chance. For if it had not been for the Lord on our side where would we be?—Thank God, He is the God of another chance. For where sin abounded grace did much more abound—Thank God, He is the God of another, another, another, and another chance.

FOR REFLECTION

1. The focus of this sermon is on new beginnings. Can you think of a time when you have extended another chance to someone who has wronged you?

_____

_____

_____

2. Can you think of a situation, recently or not so recently, when someone has been reluctant to extend a new beginning, or another chance, to you? How did that make you feel?

_____

_____

_____

3. Why was Jonah so upset that God had extended another chance to Nineveh?

_____

_____

_____

4. What was it about Jonah that caused God to give him a second chance? What was it about the Ninevites that caused God to persist in sending Jonah to them?

_____

_____

_____

5. Do you believe God will always be the God of a second chance? What in God's nature would cause Him to change? What in God's nature would cause Him to remain the same?

_____

_____

_____

Chapter Eight

THE GOD OF ANOTHER CHANCE, PT. II
JONAH 3:1-10

The word of the LORD came to Jonah a second time, saying, "Get up, go to Nineveh, that great city, and proclaim to it the message that I tell you." So Jonah set out and went to Nineveh, according to the word of the LORD. Now Nineveh was an exceedingly large city, a three days' walk across. Jonah began to go into the city, going a day's walk. And he cried out, "Forty days more, and Nineveh shall be overthrown!" And the people of Nineveh believed God; they proclaimed a fast, and everyone, great and small, put on sackcloth. When the news reached the king of Nineveh, he rose from his throne, removed his robe, covered himself with sackcloth, and sat in ashes. Then he had a proclamation made in Nineveh: "By the decree of the king and his nobles: No human being or animal, no herd or flock, shall taste anything. They shall not feed, nor shall they drink water. Human beings and animals shall be covered with sackcloth, and they shall cry mightily to God. All shall turn from their evil ways and from the violence that is in their hands. Who knows? God may relent and change his mind; he may turn from his fierce anger, so that we do not perish." When God saw what they did, how they turned from their evil ways, God changed his mind about the calamity that he had said he would bring upon them; and he did not do it.

I am convinced that the stories and events given to us in the Bible were not meant to remain locked up in the past. Rather, these stories and events speak to us today and provide us with the hope we need to overcome the challenges we face in life. For instance, the story of Moses and the people of Israel, who stood with the pharaoh and his army behind them and the Red Sea before them, teaches us that if we trust God, God can make a way out of no way. The story of David slaying Goliath teaches us that when we are confronted with giants in our lives, the God we serve knows how to knock them down and to remove obstacles that stand in our way. Or, what about the story of the three Hebrew boys who were placed in a fiery furnace? That story teaches us that God is able to protect and deliver us when we find ourselves in fiery situations that can cost us our lives. Yes, I am convinced that the stories and events we read in the Bible provide us with the hope we need to overcome the challenges we face in life. The truth is, whatever we go through often prepares us for greater challenges that lay before us. Jonah's pilgrimage illustrates this truth.

God calls Jonah a second time. Even though he has tried to run and has been disobedient to the call, God has not disqualified him, given up on him, or caused him to be the "prophet on the shelf." Jonah's second call reminds us that serving God is not based on our past achievements or failures but rather the grace of God, our repentance, and our willingness to obey Him. Furthermore, after all that Jonah has been through, who better to send to Nineveh than Jonah? He is a man who knows something about God's grace and mercy.

Jonah gets a second chance and this time the text says, "So Jonah set out and went to Nineveh, according to the word of the LORD" (3:3). Now that Jonah has been through what he has been through, he realizes that obedience is better than sacrifice. He learns obedience through the things that he has suffered. Jonah is going to the wicked city of Nineveh with all of its sin, debauchery, malice, lasciviousness, hatred, cruelty, and evil. After what he experienced on a boat the last time, this time he doesn't catch a boat. Instead, he makes the long walk to the sinful city of Nineveh. How could one man confront approximately 175,000 people with a message of judgment? How could a Jew, who worships God, convince idolatrous Gentiles to believe what he has to say? How could one man reach thousands of people in a city that would take three days to cover? Well, none of this was Jonah's problem. All Jonah was required to do was what God told him to do: go preach. We waste time trying to figure out how God is going to make sense out of our mess, bad circumstances, or failed relationships when that is not for us to figure out. We do the possible, and we let God do the impossible. We preach, we pray, we fast, we seek God's face, we trust, and let God do the rest. While we are trying to figure it out, God has already worked it out. Because God is omniscient, God has already walked down the corridor of time and written the end of our story, and God always writes a good ending.

Jonah goes to Nineveh, and he preaches the message God gave him. It's a short sermon that's right to the point. It only

contained five to eight words, depending on your transla-
tion. "Forty days more, and Nineveh shall be overthrown!"
(v. 4). That's it! No nice introduction, thesis, antithesis,
relevant question, three points, or synthesis. In essence,
Jonah tells this arrogant and prideful crowd: "You better
get your act together because in forty days you are history."
Mind you, the people in Nineveh are powerful. They could
have taken Jonah out for telling them to repent while they
were waddling in their sins. But God is right there with
Jonah holding him while his knees are shaking as he does
what God told him to do and what he thought he could
not do. Let me tell you that when we are faced with a challenging task to perform for God, we must remember we
are never alone. We may not see God with our natural eye,
yet God is right there holding us, and the angels in heaven
are shouting as we do what God has told us to do. "Forty
days more, and Nineveh shall be overthrown!" In the Bible,
the number forty is often identified with judgment, divine
activity, and testing.

During the time of Noah, it rained forty days and forty
nights.

The people of Israel explored Canaan for forty days.

The nation of Israel wandered in the wilderness forty years.

Goliath taunted the army of Israel forty days, and the Lord
gave the people of Nineveh forty days to repent.

Wrapped up with this message of judgment, however, is a
message of love, grace, and mercy. You see, God gave Nineveh
forty days to repent. Because of their wickedness, God was
not obligated to give them any time. God could have simply
destroyed them without warning. They had lived the way
they did for a long time. But sending Jonah to warn them

was a sign of God's love, grace, and mercy. However, while God was preparing Jonah to go to Nineveh, God also must have in some way prepared the Ninevites' hearts to receive the word from the prophet. When Jonah finished preaching, the people believed God, proclaimed a fast, and put on sackcloth. When the word got to the king of Nineveh, he arose from his throne, laid aside his robe, covered himself with sackcloth and sat in ashes and caused everyone, including the animals, to fast. Sackcloth was a dark cloth made from the long hairs of goats and camels. It had a coarse and itchy texture. Its darkness expressed the sorrow one felt. Being coarse and itchy symbolized the humility, shame, and discomfort of one's sin. Nineveh fasted in order to pursue spiritual matters and wore sackcloth to demonstrate the awfulness and shame of their sin.

The king asked in verse nine, "Who knows? God may relent and change his mind; he may turn from his fierce anger, so that we do not perish." In essence he was saying, "Who knows? If we do what God tells us to do, demonstrate our remorse and repent, God may extend mercy for God moves in mysterious ways." Let me tell you, in case you forgot, that God is merciful. How do I know? When we should be down, He lifts us up. When we should be crazy, He keeps us in perfect peace. When we should be broke, He supplies all of our needs. When we are in trouble, He delivers us. When we should be condemned, He rescues and saves us. The text says, "And when God saw their works, that they turned from their evil way; and God repented of the evil that he had said that he would do upon them; and he did it not" (v. 10, KJV). Even though the text says, Nineveh believed, it was when God saw their works, fasting and putting on sackcloth, that God saved them. Faith without works is dead.

Theologically, we can debate over the issue of whether or not God changes His mind. We may answer this with certain Scripture verses. James says, "Every generous act of giving, with every perfect gift, is from above, coming down from the Father of lights, with whom there is no variation or shadow due to change" (1:17). Malachi quotes God saying, "For I the LORD do not change…." (3:6). The author of Hebrews says, "Jesus Christ is the same yesterday and today and forever" (13:3). Did God change His mind when it came to destroying Nineveh? No! God did not change His mind. Nineveh changed her ways, and God did what God does whenever God's people repent, and that is, God demonstrates love, grace, and mercy. The good news is, if God can forgive wicked, sinful, and malicious Nineveh because of her repentance, then God is saying to all of us there is hope for us, too, if we turn to Him.

One last thing I need to bring out. Notice what God had to take Jonah through to get him where He wanted him. Once Jonah preached to Nineveh, it appears that they immediately repented. God sent the right prophet to Nineveh. You see even though Jonah's sermon was short, it was Jonah's life experience that was the real sermon. Jonah was a sign to Nineveh as to what can happen when we disobey God. No doubt, Nineveh heard how Jonah was caught in a storm because of his disobedience, thrown overboard, sinking in raging water, swallowed by a fish, and vomited on dry land. To see Jonah still standing and preaching with power and passion was a testimony that God is the God of another chance. Jonah could say to Nineveh, without even opening his mouth, "When you see me and all the mess I've been through and I am still standing, God is a God of another chance."

God kept Jonah, God kept Nineveh, and God will keep us in the midst of it all because He is a God of another, and another, and another chance.

FOR REFLECTION

1. Dr. Croft begins this sermon with a meditation on the power of stories to move people. How have stories (from any source) moved you to take action in your life?

_____

_____

2. Why is Jonah's sermon, as recounted in the narrative, so short? Do you think he said more that was simply not included in the Bible? In what other ways might he have called Nineveh to repentance?

_____

_____

3. Consider the king's question: "Who knows? God may relent and change his mind; he may turn from his fierce anger, so that we do not perish" (Jon. 3:9). What is behind the

king's question? Frustration? Fear? Hope?

_____

_____

_____

4. Jonah's message worked, and the people of Nineveh repented. How does a sure victory encourage obedience to your calling? What would failure in a calling mean to you?

_____

_____

_____

5. When has God given you a second chance? What did He want you to do or where did He want you go?

_____

_____

_____

6. Have you ever ignored God's second chance? If so, why? What do you need in order to be obedient to God's first call?

_____

_____

_____

Chapter Nine

A LESSON ON GRACE
JONAH 4:1-11

But this was very displeasing to Jonah, and he became angry. He prayed to the LORD and said, 'O LORD! Is not this what I said while I was still in my own country? That is why I fled to Tarshish at the beginning; for I knew that you are a gracious God and merciful, slow to anger, and abounding in steadfast love, and ready to relent from punishing. And now, O LORD, please take my life from me, for it is better for me to die than to live.' And the LORD said, 'Is it right for you to be angry?' Then Jonah went out of the city and sat down east of the city, and made a booth for himself there. He sat under it in the shade, waiting to see what would become of the city. The LORD God appointed a bush, and made it come up over Jonah, to give shade over his head, to save him from his discomfort; so Jonah was very happy about the bush. But when dawn came up the next day, God appointed a worm that attacked the bush, so that it withered. When the sun rose, God prepared a sultry east wind, and the sun beat down on the head of Jonah so that he was

*faint and asked that he might die. He said, 'It is better for me
to die than to live.' But God said to Jonah, 'Is it right for you
to be angry about the bush?' And he said, 'Yes, angry enough to
die.' Then the LORD said, 'You are concerned about the bush, for
which you did not labour and which you did not grow; it came
into being in a night and perished in a night. And should I not
be concerned about Nineveh, that great city, in which there are
more than a hundred and twenty thousand people who do not
know their right hand from their left,. and also many animals?*

*J*n the introduction to his book on Jonah, O.S.
Hawkins provides us with some headlines for each
chapter that highlight the prophet Jonah's pilgrimage. Over the first chapter of Jonah, Hawkins says
we can write the word *rejection.* God called Jonah to go to
Nineveh and to be the agent of revival. Jonah, however, went
in the opposite direction, choosing to reject the will of God
for his life. Many of us find ourselves living in chapter one
and rejecting God's claim on our lives. Over chapter two,
we can write the word *reflection.* It is in the belly of the fish
Jonah begins to reflect and pray. This is where some of us find
ourselves. We have to suffer before we surrender to God's
will, and the adversities, trials, and troubles of life find their
way of bringing us to a moment of reflection. Over chapter
three we can write the word *correction.* As Jonah sits on the
shore, having been delivered from the belly of the fish, chapter three says that, "the word of the LORD came to Jonah a
second time" (v. 1). Jonah got up, obeyed the word of God,
went to Nineveh and a mighty revival occurred. Jonah cor-
rected his ways. Finally, Hawkins says that chapter four we
can write the word *objection.*[60] The fourth chapter is a difficult

one both to understand and to preach. One would think that after describing Nineveh's repentance and revival in chapter three, chapter four would tell us about Jonah rejoicing and leaping for joy, but such is not the case.

If the book of Jonah had ended at the last verse of chapter three, history would have portrayed Jonah as the greatest prophet-preacher that ever lived. It would have been highly appropriate for Jonah to end or conclude the book that bears his name at chapter three. But Jonah goes on to tell us about his displeasure and his objection to what God has done. He tells us about his anger. He shares with us another side of himself that to the spiritual eye is not pleasant. I like Jonah for his willingness to be honest about how he felt. He teaches us that we can be honest with God about how we feel and that, in spite of our failures and faults, God can still use us. The Bible, as highly as we esteem it—and we should—does not hide or cover up any of the flaws of its heroes and heroines. It tells us about:

Noah who had a drinking problem
Abraham who lied
Sarah who had doubts
Moses who had a stammering tongue
Elijah who suffered from depression
David who had a man murdered
Jeremiah who had suicidal thoughts
Peter who was prideful
Paul who had a thorn in his flesh
However, through Jonah's flaws, faults, and anger, God demonstrated His grace.

Jonah is angry because he did exactly what God asked of him. He went to Nineveh and told the Ninevites, "Yet forty days and Nineveh will be overthrown." Nineveh repented and God relented from destroying them. What Jonah thought was going to happen and what he wanted to happen, did not happen.

At this point Jonah perhaps thought of the words of Deuteronomy 18, which says the way to test if a prophet speaks in the name of the Lord or if they are a true or false prophet is determined by whether or not their prophecy comes true (see vv. 21-22). Jonah's prophecy and proclamation, in his mind, didn't come true, so he became angry with God because he looked like a false prophet. He has been bamboozled. Jonah was angry. The truth is, there have been times in our lives when things didn't work out the way we wanted them to and we, like Jonah, became angry with God. However, because of our reverence and holy fear of God we may not have called it anger. We use other words—we say that we are *upset, questioning,* or *disappointed* with what God has decided to do. In reality we are angry. When God takes our loved ones unexpectedly. When we are constantly overlooked for a job or promotion. When the cancer we thought was in remission comes back. When our enemies, who do not know the Lord, seem to be prospering. When our godly marriage or relationship hits rock bottom and we feel that we have done everything God has told us to do. When our love is not reciprocated and bitterness is the order of the day. Sometimes it's hard to yield to the sovereignty of God and because of this, we become angry. Jonah prophesied about the imminent doom of Nineveh and doom had not come.

Jonah, the indignant prophet prayed to the Lord and said, "I knew it! I knew all the time you were going to relent. That's why I ran the first time and went in the opposite direction. I knew you were gracious and merciful, slow to anger, abounding in loving kindness and one who relents from doing harm" (see vv. 1-2). Jonah's mad, but he's praying and praising God for His attributes. Here's a lesson that Jonah teaches us. Although his prayer is not a good one as he asks God to take his life, he is still talking to God. You might be upset with God but keep talking to God because the more you talk to God, the more you'll see how good He really is in spite of your let down. And even when you are mad at God, if you have a good relationship with Him in your anger, you'll end up praising Him because behind the tragedy is a God that loves you and knows what's best. Yes God, in spite of what has happened, You are gracious, merciful, slow to anger, abundant in love, and One who relents from doing harm.

Yes, the Lord was gracious but not only was His grace extended to Nineveh, it was also extended to Jonah. Jonah was so upset that he asked God to take his life. God however was patient and gracious with Jonah. For if God had been one of the lesser gods he would have wiped Jonah out on the spot. The truth is, there is a little of Jonah in all of us. We've all done something and said some things that gave God the right to finish us off. Nowhere in this book can we look down on Jonah because all of us have felt what Jonah felt and all of us are recipients of God's grace.

Look at what God does! Jonah goes out of the city, sits on the east side, thinking that because he brought his case to God, God will now destroy Nineveh. Jonah builds himself a shelter and waits to see what will become of Nineveh. The weather was hot on the east side, but the text says that the Lord prepared a bush to give him shade for his head. The bush was likely the castor bean plant that grew in the sandy regions of the Middle East. It had large leaves and grew to a considerable height in just a few days. God sheltered Jonah. In the first chapter when Jonah was being disobedient and almost drowned, God prepared a great fish to swallow Jonah. When Jonah was angry and wanted to die, chapter four says that God prepared a plant to shelter him. God kept protecting and covering Jonah when he was in danger and when he was a danger to himself. If we, too, looked back over our lives we would see that God always provided us with what we needed even when we were disobedient and acting crazy. Yes, God keeps us even when we don't want to be kept, saving us from ourselves.

But just like God prepared the plant that Jonah was excited and grateful for, the next morning God prepared a worm that damaged the plant and caused it to wither. Jonah didn't realize he needed the worm so that he might look to God and thank God for the worm too. God protects us from ourselves by removing plants that occupy the center of our attention when God wants the center of our attention to be His will. When God removes plants from our lives, He allows us to see how dependent we've become on things rather than Him.

Jonah, however, was mad and angry that God destroyed the plant. God asked Jonah a question. "Is it right for you to be angry about a plant when Nineveh which consists of 120,000 people cannot tell right from wrong are being saved and experiencing my grace? Jonah, have you forgotten that quick how I have dealt with you? I could have cut you off when you were on your way to Tarshish, but I didn't. I could have let you drown when those sailors threw you overboard, but I didn't. I didn't have to prepare a fish to protect you when you went deliberately walking contrary to my will, but I did. I responded to you with love, mercy, grace, patience, and pardon in spite of your rebellion. Should I not do the same for Nineveh? Let me give you a lesson on grace."

Ken Langley and his wife were at an airport worried that they wouldn't be able to board an overbooked flight. A half an hour later, they were summoned to the check-in desk. The flight agent told them this was their lucky day; they were being bumped to first class. This was the first time they had flown first class and had been pampered on an airplane—good food, hot coffee, and plenty of elbowroom. They decided, while in first class, to play a game. They tried to guess who else didn't belong in first class. They noticed a man who walked around the cabin in his socks—didn't belong. A woman sampling magazines—didn't belong. Someone who kept playing with the flight phone but never used it—didn't belong. When the Langleys thought about it, as much as those individuals did not belong in first class, neither did they. They came to see that the same grace that had been extended to them must be shown to those who are still in coach to help them experience God's first class grace.

Jonah, grace is not just for you. It's also for the young woman who sells her body in exchange for money; the boy standing on the corner doing what is not right; the man who keeps making the wrong decisions; the person who is smoking away their life. It's for Nineveh, for you, and for me. That's why we call it "Amazing Grace" because God's grace is so amazing. I thank God grace came my way. I don't deserve it, but I'm glad God offers it. It's "amazing grace how sweet the sound that saved a wretch like me. I once was lost but now I'm found, was blind but now I see." I don't know about you but "Amazing Grace" will always be my song of praise. For it was grace that brought me liberty. I do not know just why He came to love me so. He looked beyond my faults and saw my need. I shall forever lift mine eyes to Calvary, to view the cross, where Jesus died for me. How marvelous, His grace that caught my falling soul. He looked beyond my faults and saw my need. Yes, grace woke me up this morning. Grace started me on my way. Grace will make you love your enemies. Grace will brighten your day and grace will give you the victory.

Always remember that God calls us unexpectedly to go to unexpected places, but He never calls us or sends us without His grace. That's a lesson on grace!

FOR REFLECTION

1. Can you think of a time when you have been indignant over someone else's success or favor? How were you able to move past those feelings?

_____

_____

_____

2. What are some of the most important lessons that you will take away from this series of sermons? What have they taught you about God?

_____

_____

_____

NOTES

[1]I will use the terms *black* and *African-American* interchangeably to refer to people of African descent, their church, and preacher. These terms refer to the descendants of a relative handful of black indentured servants and the estimated ten to eleven million slaves who arrived in the United States during the colonial and antebellum periods. Although the term *African-American* is the most popular term today, there also remains some preference for the term *black*. Second, in using the terms *black church* or *African-American church*, I speak of a church which is predominantly made up of people who are of African descent and whose worship style displays certain characteristics.

[2]Marvin A. McMickle, *Where Have All the Prophets Gone? Reclaiming Prophetic Preaching in America* (Cleveland: Pilgrim Press, 2006).

[3]Joseph Faulkner, "What Are They Saying? A Content Analysis of 206 Sermons Preached in the Christian Church (Disciples of Christ) during 1988," in *A Case Study of Mainstream Protestantism: The Disciples' Relation to American Culture, 1880-1989*, ed. D. Newell Williams (St. Louis: Chalice Press and Grand Rapids: Eerdmans, 1991), 416-439.

[4]Marsha Witten, *All Is Forgiven: The Secular Message of American Protestantism* (Princeton: Princeton University Press, 1995), 34-53.

[5]Cleophus J. LaRue, *The Heart of Black Preaching* (Louisville: Westminster John Knox Press, 2000), 22.

[6]Martin Luther King, Jr., *Strength to Love* (New York: Harper & Row, 1963), 43.

[7]Samuel D. Proctor, "Prophetic Preaching Now: A Generation after King," in *Preaching on the Brink: The Future of Homiletics*, ed. Martha J. Simmons (Nashville: Abingdon Press, 1996), 154.

[8]Ibid., 156-157.

[9]J. Philip Wogaman, *Speaking the Truth in Love: Prophetic Preaching to a Broken World* (Louisville: Westminster John Knox Press, 1998), 4, 7.

[10]Ronald J. Allen, "The Relationship Between the Pastoral and the Prophetic in Preaching," *Encounter* 49.3 (1988): 173.

[11]Kelly Miller Smith, *Social Crisis Preaching* (Macon: Mercer University Press, 1984), 33.

[12]McMickle, 12.

[13]See Donald K. McKim, *Westminster Dictionary of Theological Terms* (Louisville: Westminster John Knox Press, 1996), 176, 214; Heath White, *Post-Modernism 101* (Grand Rapids: Brazos Press, 2006), 12-13.

[14]Sarah K. Asaftei, "Belonging Before Believing: Reaching Out to the Emerging Culture," *Ministry* (January 2007): 22. Online: *http://www.ministrymagazine.org/archive/2007/january/belonging-before-believing.html.*

[15]Diogenes Allen, *Christian Belief in a Postmodern World: The Full Wealth of Conviction* (Louisville: Westminster John Knox Press, 1989), 8.

[16]Craig A. Loscalzo, *Apologetic Preaching: Proclaiming Christ to a Postmodern World* (Downers Grove: InterVarsity Press, 2000), 18.

[17]David Buttrick, *A Captive Voice: The Liberation of Preaching* (Louisville: Westminster John Knox Press, 1994), 111-112.

[18]See Robert Kysar and Joseph Webb, *Preaching to Postmoderns* (Peabody: Hendrickson Publishers, 2006), xx-xxix; White, 23-38.

[19]Cleophus J. LaRue, *I Believe I'll Testify: The Art of African American Preaching* (Louisville: Westminster John Knox Press, 2011), 61.

[20]LaRue, *Heart of Black Preaching,* 6.

[21]LaRue, *I Believe I'll Testify,* 61.

[22]See Luke 4:16-21.

[23]Allen, 65.

[24]Abraham Heschel, *The Prophets,* 3rd. ed. (Peabody: Hendrickson Publishers, 2000); Walter Brueggemann, *The Prophetic Imagination,* 2nd ed. (Minneapolis: Fortress Press, 2001).

[25]Efrem Smith and Phil Jackson, *The Hip-Hop Church: Connecting with the Movement Shaping Our Culture* (Downers Grove: InterVarsity Press, 2005), 105.

[26]"Bush Doesn't Care About Black People," Online: *http://www.youtube.com/watch?v=zIUzLpO1kxI&NR.* Accessed 10 July 2012.

[27]Smith and Jackson, 112.

[28]James Ward and Christine Ward, *Preaching from the Prophets* (Nashville: Abingdon Press, 1995), 11.

[29]Graham Johnston, *Preaching to a Postmodern World: A Guide to Reaching Twenty-First Century Listeners* (Grand Rapids: Baker Books, 2001), 87-88.

[30]James Melvin Washington, *Frustrated Fellowship: The Black Baptist Quest for Social Power* (Macon: Mercer University Press, 1986), ix.

[31]Ward, 53.

[32]Walter Brueggemann, *Hope Within History* (Atlanta: John Knox Press, 1987), 74.

[33]Wogaman, 82.

[34]James H. Cone, *Black Theology and Black Power*, New Ed. (Maryknoll, NY: Orbis, 1999), 31-61.

[35]Ibid., 126.

[36]Ibid., 127.

[37]William B. McClain, *Come Sunday: The Liturgy of Zion* (Nashville: Abingdon Press, 1990), 62-70.

[38]Ibid., 68-69.

[39]LaRue, *Heart of Black Preaching*, 3.

[40]"It Will Surely Come," Online: *http://www.csec.org/index.php/component/content/article/23-member-archives/453-cleophus-larue-program-4517?highlight=YTozOntpOjA7czo4OiJjbGVucGh1cyI7aToxO3M6NToibGFydWUiO2k6MjtzOjE0OiJjbGVucGh1cyBsYXJ1ZSI7fQ==*

[41]LaRue, *Heart of Black Preaching*, 14.

[42]Ibid., 15.

[43]Henry H. Mitchell, *Black Preaching: The Recovery of a Powerful Art*, (Nashville: Abingdon Press, 1990), 130.

[44]Ibid., 131.

[45]William M. Pickard, *Rather Die than Live—Jonah* (New York: Board of Global Ministries, The United Methodist Church, 1974), 18.

[46]Henry H. Mitchell, *Recovery of Preaching* (San Francisco: Harper & Row, 1977), 54.

[47]Ibid., 133.

[48]Olin P. Moyd, *The Sacred Art: Preaching and Theology in the African American Tradition* (Valley Forge: Judson Press, 1995), 108-11.

[49]Frank A. Thomas, *They Like To Never Quit Praisin' God: The Role of Celebration In Preaching* (Cleveland: United Church Press, 1997), 85; Henry H. Mitchell, *Celebration and Experience in Preaching* (Nashville: Abingdon

Press, 1990), 12.

[50]Mitchell, *Black Preaching*, 120-21.

[51]The author of this traditional song is unknown; however, it is often heard in African-American churches in America.

[52]*Christianity Today*, 1993.

[53]Harold A. Carter, *The Preaching of Jonah: Evangelistic Messages for our Contemporary World* (Elgin: Progressive Baptist Publishing House, 1981), 5.

[54]John Phillips, *Exploring the Minor Prophets: An Exploratory Commentary* (Grand Rapids: Kregel Publications, 1998), 141.

[55]O. S. Hawkins, *Jonah: Meeting the God of the Second Chance* (Neptune: Loizeaux Brothers, Inc., 1990), 31.

[56]Isaac Watts, "At the Cross," in *The New National Baptist Hymnal* (Nashville: National Baptist Publishing Board, 1983), 79.

[57]Oliver Ernesto Branch, ed., *The Hamilton Speaker* (1878), 53.

[58]Ernest W. Blandy, "Where He Leads Me," in *The New National Baptist Hymnal* (Nashville: National Baptist Publishing Board, 1983), 168.

[59]Joseph A. Scriven, "What A Friend We Have in Jesus," in *The New National Baptist Hymnal* (Nashville: National Baptist Publishing Board, 1983), 340.

[60]O. S. Hawkins, *Jonah: Meeting the God of the Second Chance*, 16-18.

BIBLIOGRAPHY

Achtemeier, Elizabeth. *Preaching from the Minor Prophets: Text and Sermon Suggestions.* Grand Rapids, MI: Eerdmans, 1998.

Allen, Diogenes. *Christian Belief in a Postmodern World: The Full Wealth of Conviction.* Louisville: Westminster John Knox Press, 1989.

Allen, Leslie C. *The Books of Joel, Obadiah, Jonah, and Micah.* New International Commentary on the Old Testament. Grand Rapids, MI: Eerdmans, 1976.

Allen, Ronald J. "The Relationship Between the Pastoral and the Prophetic in Preaching." *Encounter* 49.3 (1988): 173-89.

Alling, Roger and David J. Schlafer, eds. *Preaching as Prophetic Calling: Sermons that Work XII.* Harrisburg, PA: Morehouse Publishing, 2004.

Boice, James Montgomery. *The Minor Prophets: Hosea-Jonah.* An Expositional Commentary. Grand Rapids, MI: Baker, 2006.

Borschel, Audrey. *Preaching Prophetically When the News Disturbs: Interpreting the Media.* St. Louis, MO: Chalice Press, 2009.

Brueggemann, Walter. *Hope Within History.* Atlanta: John Knox Press, 1987.

_____. *The Prophetic Imagination.* Second Edition. Minneapolis: Augsburg Fortress Press, 2001.

Carter, Harold A. *The Preaching of Jonah: Evangelistic Messages for our Contemporary World.* Elgin, IL: Progressive Baptist Publishing House, 1981.

Cary, Phillip. *Jonah.* Brazos Theological Commentary on the Bible. Grand Rapids, MI: Brazos Press, 2008.

Clader, Linda L. *Voicing the Vision: Imagination and Prophetic Preaching.* Harrisburg, PA: Morehouse Publishing, 2003.

Cone, James H. *Black Theology and Black Power.* New Edition. Maryknoll, NY: Orbis Books, 1999.

De La Torre, Miguel A. *Liberating Jonah: Forming an Ethics of Reconciliation.* Maryknoll, NY: Orbis Books, 2007.

Ellison, H. L. *Jonah.* Expositor's Bible Commentary, Vol. 7. Grand Rapids, MI: Zondervan, 1985.

Estelle, Bryan D. *Salvation through Judgment and Mercy: The Gospel According to Jonah.* Phillipsburg, NJ: P & R Publishing, 2005.

Ferguson, Sinclair B. *Man Overboard! The Story of Jonah.* Carlisle, PA: Banner of Truth, 2008.

Fleer, David and Dave Bland, eds. *Preaching the Eighth Century Prophets.* Abilene, TX: Abilene Christian University Press, 2004.

Hawkins, O. S. *Jonah: Meeting the God of the Second Chance.* Neptune, NJ: Loizeaux Brothers, Inc., 1990.

Heschel, Abraham J. *The Prophets.* 2 vols. New York: Harper & Row, 1962.

Johnson, Kenyatta R. *The Journey and Promise of African American Preaching.* Minneapolis: Fortress Press, 2011.

Johnston, Graham. *Preaching to a Postmodern World: A Guide to Reaching Twenty-First Century Listeners.* Grand Rapids, MI: Baker, 2001.

Kendall, R. T. *Jonah.* London: Hodder & Stoughton, 1978.

Kysar, Robert and Joseph Webb, *Preaching to Postmoderns.* Peabody, MA: Hendrickson Publishers, Inc., 2006.

LaRue, Cleophus J. *The Heart of Black Preaching.* Louisville: Westminster John Knox Press, 2000.

_____. *I Believe I'll Testify: The Art of African American Preaching.* Louisville: Westminster John Knox Press, 2011.

Loscalzo, Craig A. *Apologetic Preaching: Proclaiming Christ to a Postmodern World.* Downers Grove, IL: InterVarsity Press, 2000.

McClain, William B. *Come Sunday: The Liturgy of Zion.* Nashville: Abingdon Press, 1990.

McMickle, Marvin A. *Where Have All the Prophets Gone? Reclaiming Prophetic Preaching in America.* Cleveland: Pilgrim Press, 2006.

Mitchell, Henry H. *Black Preaching.* New York: Harper & Row, 1970.

_____. *Black Preaching: The Recovery of a Powerful Art.* Nashville: Abingdon Press, 1990.

_____. *Celebration and Experience in Preaching.* Nashville: Abingdon Press, 1990.

Morris, Henry M. *The Remarkable Journey of Jonah: A Scholarly, Conservative Study of his Amazing Record.* Green Forest, AR: Master Books, 2003.

Moyd, Olin P. *Redemption in Black Theology.* Valley Forge, PA: Judson Press, 1979.

Nixon, Rosemary A. *The Message of Jonah: Presence in the Storm.* Downers Grove, IL: InterVarsity Press, 2003.

Phillips, John. *Exploring the Minor Prophets: An Expository Commentary.* Grand Rapids, MI: Kregel Publications, 1998.

Pickard, William M. *Rather Die than Live—Jonah.* New York: Board of Global Ministries, The United Methodist Church, 1974.

Proctor, Samuel D. "Prophetic Preaching Now: A Generation after King," in *Preaching on the Brink: The Future of Homiletics,* ed. Martha J. Simmons. Nashville: Abingdon Press, 1996.

Seed, Hal. *Jonah: Responding to God in all the Right Ways.* Dayton, OH: New Song Press, 2008.

Smith, Efrem and Phil Jackson, *The Hip-Hop Church: Connecting with the Movement Shaping Our Culture.* Downers Grove, IL: InterVarsity Press, 2005.

Stevenson, John. *Preaching from the Minor Prophets: To a Postmodern Congregation.* Southfield, MI: Redeemer Publishing, 2008.

Tchividjian, Tullian. *Surprised by Grace: God's Relentless Pursuit of Rebels.* Wheaton, IL: Crossway, 2010.

The New National Baptist Hymnal. Nashville: National Baptist Publishing Board, 1983.

Thomas, Frank A. *They Like To Never Quit Praisin' God: The Role of Celebration In Preaching.* Cleveland: United Church Press, 1997.

Tubbs-Tisdale, Lenora. *Prophetic Preaching: A Pastoral Approach.* Louisville: Westminster John Knox Press, 2010.

Smith, Kelly Miller. *Social Crisis Preaching: The Lyman Beecher Lectures 1983.* Macon, GA: Mercer University Press, 1984.

Ward, James, and Christine Ward. *Preaching from the Prophets.* Nashville: Abingdon Press, 1995.

Washington, James Melvin. *Frustrated Fellowship: The Black Baptist Quest for Social Power.* Macon, GA: Mercer University Press, 1986.

Wogaman, J. Philip. *Speaking the Truth in Love: Prophetic Preaching to a Broken World.* Louisville: Westminster John Knox Press, 1998.

ABOUT THE AUTHOR

Wayne E. Croft, Sr. serves as the pastor of the St. Paul's Baptist Church in West Chester, Pennsylvania. St. Paul's is the oldest Baptist Church of African-American heritage in Chester County, Pennsylvania. Prior to being called to St. Paul's Dr. Croft served for nineteen years as the pastor of The Church of the Redeemer, Baptist, in Philadelphia.

Dr. Croft has also served as Assistant Professor of Homiletics and Liturgics at Palmer Theological Seminary of Eastern University in Philadelphia and now serves as the Jeremiah A. Wright, Sr. Associate Professor of Homiletics and Liturgics in African-American Studies at Lutheran Theological Seminary in Philadelphia and as Christian Education Director of the Pennsylvania Eastern Keystone Baptist Association. Dr. Croft is the founder of the Redeemer Renaissance Community Development Corporation, a life member of the Kappa Alpha Psi Fraternity, Inc., and has been inducted into the Martin Luther King, Jr. Board of Preachers of Morehouse College in Atlanta, Georgia. *The African American Pulpit* Journal (Winter 2007-2008) recognized him as one of the top twenty–two revivalists in the African-American church. *The African-American Pulpit* also published his sermons:

"The Promise Guaranteed" (Summer 1999), "A Candidate for the Hall of Faith" (Winter 2008-2009), and his article titled "What Does It Mean to Preach Biblically Today?" (Winter 2003). He is a contributor to the book, *From One Brother to Another: Voices of African-American Men, Volume II* (Judson Press) and has further published two articles in the Past Master section of *Preaching Magazine*: "John Jasper: Preaching with Authority" and "E. K. Bailey: Expositor of the Word."

Dr. Croft is a graduate of Pinebrook Junior College where he earned an associate degree and graduated *magna cum laude* from Trinity College earning his Bachelor of Arts. He earned the Master of Divinity from Eastern Baptist Theological Seminary (now Palmer Theological Seminary), the Master of Theology from Princeton Theological Seminary, and graduated with distinction from Drew University earning a Doctor of Ministry. He also earned a Master of Philosophy degree from Drew University and a Doctor of Philosophy from Drew University in Madison, New Jersey. Dr. Croft is married to Dr. Lisa L. Croft, a family physician. They have three children: Darlene (presently a law student at North Carolina Central University), Wayne Jr., and Candace Nicole.

www.ingramcontent.com/pod-product-compliance
Lightning Source LLC
LaVergne TN
LVHW021522080426
835509LV00018B/2602